GEOPHILOSOPHY

On Gilles Deleuze and Félix Guattari's *What Is Philosophy?*

Rodolphe Gasché

Northwestern University Press
Evanston, Illinois

Northwestern University Press
www.nupress.northwestern.edu

Printed in the United States of America
10 9 8 7 6 5 4 3 2 1

Library of Congress Cataloging-in-Publication Data
Gasché, Rodolphe, author.
Geophilosophy : on Gilles Deleuze and Felix Guattari's What is philosophy? / Rodolphe Gasché.
pages cm. — (Northwestern University studies in comparative and continental philosophy)
"This book in the main consists of lectures that I first delivered in 2010 at the Collegium Phenomenologicum at Citta di Castello, Italy, and subsequently expanded for a three-day seminar at the Universidad Diego Portales at Santiago, Chile, in 2011. In spring 2012 my graduate lecture course in the Department of Comparative Literature at the State University of New York at Buffalo was devoted to the subject 'geophilosophy.' It was on this occasion that I expanded the earlier lectures to the dimensions of the book in its present form."
ISBN 978-0-8101-2944-3 (pbk.) — ISBN 978-0-8101-2972-6 (cloth)
1. Deleuze, Gilles, 1925–1995. Qu'est-ce que la philosophie? 2. Guattari, Félix, 1930–1992. 3. Philosophy. 4. Earth (Planet)—Philosophy. 5. Science. 6. Logic. I. Title. II. Series: Northwestern University studies in comparative and continental philosophy.
B2430.D453Q4734 2014
100—dc23

2013025592

♾ The paper used in this publication meets the minimum requirements of the American National Standard for Information Sciences—Permanence of Paper for Printed Library Materials, ANSI Z39.48-1992.

GEOPHILOSOPHY

Studies in Comparative

and

Continental Philosophy

Series Editors David Jones
Michael Schwartz
Jason Wirth

Contents

Acknowledgments

This book in the main consists of lectures that I first delivered in 2010 at the Collegium Phenomenologicum at Citta di Castello, Italy, and subsequently expanded for a three-day seminar at the Universidad Diego Portales at Santiago, Chile, in 2011. In spring 2012 my graduate lecture course in the Department of Comparative Literature at the State University of New York at Buffalo was devoted to the subject "geophilosophy." It was on this occasion that I expanded the earlier lectures to the dimensions of the book in its present form. In summer 2012, I tested the ideas presented in chapters 2 and 3 one last time during a workshop on geophilosophy at the Zentrum für Literatur- und Kulturforschung in Berlin, Germany.

I am indebted to all who attended those lectures, seminars, and workshops, and who provided me with constructive feedback as I was bringing these investigations to a conclusion. Grateful thanks are due to Donald Cross, who helped me a great deal with editing and preparing the manuscript for publication. But above all I want to thank Bronia Karst for her patience and encouragement throughout the time I worked on this project. I cannot thank her enough.

Introduction

What Is Philosophy?, the last work published under the names of both Gilles Deleuze and Félix Guattari, was, as their biographer, François Dosse, acknowledges, "written somewhat differently than the earlier books."[1] It "was manifestly written by Deleuze alone, but he agreed to a coauthor credit with Guattari, as a tribute to their exceptionally intense friendship, suggesting too that the ideas developed in the book and its language were the fruit of their common endeavors since 1969."[2] In the following commentary on *What Is Philosophy?,* if I use the abbreviation D&G to refer to both authors rather than each time spelling their names in full, it is not only for reasons of economy but also to honor their friendship and to pay tribute to the fact that Guattari suggested some revisions and defined new directions, working, apparently, from the manuscript that Deleuze sent him. But perhaps more important than the fact that the work was written primarily by Deleuze himself, the project to write a book on *What Is Philosophy?* was conceived by Deleuze after D&G had published *A Thousand Plateaus.* Dosse writes: "Indeed, ever since *A Thousand Plateaus,* Deleuze had been saying that he wanted to work on this theme; his closing words to his final class at Paris-VIII in 1980 were, 'Next year, I have to find something new. My dream would be a course on "what is philosophy?"' His students thought he was joking and broke out laughing. During the 1980s, Deleuze repeated this to his students, saying he had never managed to do the course on philosophy because he was not yet ready to answer that question."[3] Several other statements, such as that in a letter to Guattari from 1981, or his comment in an interview from 1988 following the publication of *The Fold* that he "want(s) to write a book on 'What Is Philosophy?,'" indicate that the project to address this question was continuously on Deleuze's mind.[4] Dosse's observation that *What Is Philosophy?* is "both a very personal project and something of a crowning moment in a philosopher's life"[5] is thus to the point. Indeed, according to the first sentences of the book, the question "what is philosophy?" is one that "can perhaps be posed only late in life," after having done philosophy all one's life without ever having had the leisure of explicitly reflecting on what it is that one has been doing, and, "when there is no longer anything to ask," the question "what is philosophy?" is the crowning question in the life of the philosopher.[6]

The reading of *What Is Philosophy?* that I propose hereafter does not intend to establish what Deleuze's or, for that matter, D&G's philosophy is. I do not pretend to have discovered the essence of their thought. By contrast, I will be interested in what they themselves define as philosophy in distinction from the sciences and the arts and what it is that they understand to have done while doing philosophy. Furthermore, I will be concerned with the authors' claim not only that philosophy is a Greek thing but also that, as such, it is, for fundamental reasons, geophilosophical in nature. Although it is only in this late work that this point is made, I will also intimate that, rather than a marginal issue of Deleuze's or D&G's conception of philosophy, a certain geocentrism is from the beginning a central dimension of his, or their, thinking. Indeed, as I will argue, if all the principal traits that constitute philosophy according to D&G—*autochthony, philia,* and *doxa*—imply in an essential manner a concern with the Earth, it follows that what Deleuze or D&G have been doing while doing philosophy has been marked by this concern from the start.

My commentary will thus focus on the concept of philosophy advanced in *What Is Philosophy?* Everything that is established with regard to the sciences and the arts will be taken up only inasmuch as it is necessary to provide a more precise account of philosophy and its intrinsic relation to the Earth. Systematic attention will therefore be given to exactly how the three traits that constitute philosophy as something Greek are grounded in this fundamental concern with the Earth. To elaborate on the three traits in question a number of detours through D&G's Greek sources and through the scholars on whose work they have relied to make their point will prove to be inevitable. Indeed, in my reading of D&G's last work I give privilege to their own sources for their thought over the enormous Deleuze scholarship, which in any case has taken up the issue of the geophilosophical, to my knowledge, only on a few occasions. Methodically speaking wherever possible, I will also retranslate their terminology back into more traditional philosophical conceptuality, instead of merely rehashing it. D&G's technical language is not self-explicatory and cannot be taken at face value. This concern with retranslating D&G's peculiar conceptuality back into more conventional terms distinguishes my reading also from Eric Alliez's *The Signature of the World, or What Is Deleuze and Guattari's Philosophy?,* the only other book that, to my knowledge, is solely devoted to *What Is Philosophy?*[7] In addition, special attention will be paid to the way D&G translate the language and conceptuality of other thinkers into their own technical idiom. To thus reconvert some of D&G's technical language back into more common, philosophical language, I have followed up on more or less the entirety of the references in the text, in the footnotes in particular, that are pertinent for their understanding of philosophy as something Greek, thus awarding to myself the necessary background not only for clarifying the statements and movements made throughout the work but also for discovering the origins and contexts of their own concepts. Such a retranslation of their singular conceptuality is, as we will see in due time, justified by D&G's own understanding of language. But such a retranslation is also warranted if one is to take seriously their claim that it is philosophy that they have been doing all their lives. Furthermore, to retranslate their often idiosyncratic terminology is a necessary move if, ultimately, one wishes to establish what, exactly, they have sought to accomplish by breaking with the classical conceptuality; in other words, such a retranslation is in principle the condition for being able to evaluate the precise contribution that their thought may make to classical philosophical problems and how it distinguishes itself from those problems. However, what this contribution effectively amounts to can only be sketched out in a dotted outline in the short study that follows.

Now, since D&G's last work forcefully heralds philosophy as a Greek thing, the task of reading *What Is Philosophy?* requires one to clearly define what it is precisely that makes philosophy an irreducibly Greek creation. But if philosophy is Greek by nature, and if, according to D&G, one has to become Greek to become a philosopher, the question that I face in my commentary on their reflection on what it is that they have been doing while doing philosophy is also how D&G have been Greek as philosophers in a time when, admittedly, it is no longer possible to be Greek. Differently worded, the question may be formulated as follows: as philosophers, how are they to become Greek in a way that is not to be confounded with what the Greeks were, so as to be able to do something different from the Greeks, something radically new, which, however, is not therefore something necessarily un-Greek, something beyond philosophy, but, on the contrary, a form of philosophy that adequately responds to the modern and contemporary world? Undoubtedly, as a reflection on what D&G have been doing throughout their lives as philosophers, *What Is Philosophy?* seeks to establish as rigorously as possible what they understand by philosophy. Yet, to the extent that the question about the essence of philosophy is framed by an inquiry into what they have been doing all their lives, *What Is Philosophy?* not only implicitly holds that all of D&G's previous work has in fact been philosophical but also establishes the outlines of a philosophy under the circumstances of the present; more precisely, it is involved in the creation of a philosophy that satisfies the milieu of contemporary democracy and capitalism. Such a philosophy in a way would still be Greek even though today one can no longer be Greek.

To return briefly to the authorship of *What Is Philosophy?*, could the fact that this work has been written by Deleuze alone be interpreted to suggest, as Dosse worries, that it is to be read as "a return to 'true' philosophy by Deleuze without Guattari"?[8] As we will see, the understanding of philosophy offered in *What Is Philosophy?* rests on a valorizing interpretation of the pre-Socratics whose thought and "truth" were already betrayed, according to the authors, by Plato's Eidetic, even before they were betrayed in the two other philosophical eras—Kant's Criticism and Husserl's Phenomenology.[9] Of course, if this last work published under the name of both authors has in fact been written by Deleuze alone, it is by a philosopher who, rather than continuing the line of classical and modern philosophy, understands "true" philosophy primarily from early Greek thought. But if Deleuze "agreed to a coauthor credit with Guattari, as a tribute to their exceptionally intense friendship, suggesting too that the ideas developed in the book and its language were the fruit of their common endeavors since 1969," is it not also because, for Deleuze, what he and Guattari had been doing all of their lives, especially when experimenting with new forms of thought that at first sight had little to do with philosophy, had always been "true" philosophy?[10] And if so, does one not, eventually, have to evaluate their work in light of this standard that they have set for themselves?

At the beginning of this introduction I said that I did not pretend to establish once and for all an exhaustive response to what the essence of Deleuze's or D&G's philosophy may be. Rather, I seek to elaborate on what they assert as the nature of philosophy as such and to tease out the presuppositions on which their redefinition of philosophy rests, as well as some of its ramifications. Although I raise a number of questions throughout this work, which in fact concludes with a battery of questions left unanswered, the thrust of this work is not critical. Its aim is to make adherence to, but also detraction of, their enterprise somewhat more complicated through a philological exploration of the resources on which they relied in defining what they understand by philosophy. Notwithstanding all the innovations that this last work, signed D&G (but also Deleuze's own last book-length study), puts forward, one of the guiding threads of my reading of *What Is Philosophy?* is that the conception of philosophy that it provides does not break with philosophy itself. Nor does the conception of philosophy offered by D&G even in the slightest way resemble a deconstruction of philosophy. Rather, *What Is Philosophy?* furnishes a conception of philosophy that only within philosophy breaks with the dominant Platonic tradition in the name of another tradition, which until more or less recently had been neglected by the tradition but, alongside the latter and in the shape of the few, discontinuous, and contingent events in which the force of "true" philosophical thought manifests itself in the long history of Western philosophy, interrupts, or punctuates, that tradition. Undoubtedly, in writing *What Is Philosophy?*, Deleuze aimed at making this last of his works into another such event.

GEOPHILOSOPHY

1

The "Greek Miracle"

In a noteworthy text that is not too well-known, "Prière sur l'Acropole," Ernest Renan recalls that his busy youth, when he was occupied with solving for himself the highest problems of philosophy and religion, did not leave him any time whatsoever to look back upon his life. Later, when forced to confront the trends of his century, which, he remarks, was as alien to him as another planet, his various occupations prevented him even further from returning in thought to a past that was of no immediate concern to him. In addition, his travels (to Syria in particular) only contributed to "further increase the distance to his old memories."[1] Indeed, Renan admits that he "began to have memories only very late." Strikingly, a highly singular experience was needed to make him even look back upon his own past in the first place. He writes: "It is a strange thing, but it was only in Athens in 1865 that I felt for the first time an intense feeling of looking back—an effect comparable to a fresh and penetrating breeze that came from far away." The sight of the Acropolis not only produces in him "an impression that was more powerful than anything he had felt before"; it also causes him to turn around, as it were, to turn back and face the past.[2] In Athens, Renan becomes aware, indeed, for the first time, of Greek antiquity as a past that, in addition to the "Jewish miracle," outflanks all contemporary concerns, a past that is of the order of a miracle, as well: the "Greek miracle." Renan avers: "For a very long time already I no longer believed in miracles in the proper sense of the word; yet the unique destiny of the Jewish people that resulted in Jesus and Christianity appeared to me to be something that stood completely apart. But now the Greek miracle came to stand for me next to the Jewish miracle, that is, a thing which existed only once, something which had never been seen before, and which one will never see again, but whose effects will last forever, I mean a type of eternal beauty, without any local or national blemish."[3] Realizing that what happened in Greece is unique and, above all, of the order of a miracle, Renan becomes interested for the first time in the past of Western culture. Before this journey to Greece he had, of course, been well aware of the fact "that Greece had created science, art, philosophy, and civilization," but it is as if this very site of a revelation of perfection comparable to no other—that is, of "the idea crystallized in Pentelican marble" on the Acropolis—and the memory of ancient Greece that it brings to life also create the conditions for Renan to turn upon himself and recollect his own past.[4] The experience of the Greek miracle, which for Renan, it seems to me, outshines even the Jewish miracle, becomes the foil against which a reflection becomes possible on what, precisely, he himself has been doing all his life while trying to solve the big questions raised by philosophy and religion. This miracle is therefore the ground for another one that interrupts Renan's activities hitherto and makes him attend to his own past. In this miracle both his personal past and the past of Europe are intertwined in such a manner that the confrontation with Europe's cultural identity in Greece becomes the condition for and modalizes the recollection of his own past.

Since Renan coined the expression, the "Greek miracle" has become a cliché of sorts that refers in particular to the rather sudden intellectual revolution of pre-Socratic thought in Ionia, during which rationalist thought emerged free from all earlier mythical and religious shackles, and the belief that this development cannot be explained simply in terms of historical and sociocultural causes.[5] In *What Is Philosophy?,* Gilles Deleuze and Félix Guattari not only employ the expression in question; they also link it, in a way similar to Renan, to a belated and recollecting reflection on their lifework as philosophers. At the very beginning of their study they remark that "the question *what is philosophy?* can perhaps be posed only late in life, with the arrival of old age and the time for speaking concretely" (1).[6] They begin to look back with the arrival of old age, wondering what it is that they have been doing all their lives while doing philosophy without reflecting on the essence of philosophy itself, on this Greek miracle, if ever there has been one (1). This gesture of reflecting at the evening of one's life on what it is, precisely, that one has been doing during one's life as a philosopher is rather conventional. Although Deleuze does not consider the owl to be among "the true philosophical beasts" (as opposed to the louse, spider, or tick), this gesture nevertheless resonates with the famous claim by Deleuze's declared archenemy, Hegel, in the preface to the *Philosophy of Right,* that the owl of Minerva, philosophy in short, takes its flight only with the setting of the sun.[7] Furthermore, by asking "what is philosophy?," D&G not only pose a specifically Greek question—the question *ti esti,* what is it?—but also inquire into the essence of something specifically Greek. Indeed, to look for what something is in its proper essence, that is, to be able to see something within the sharply highlighted limits of its outlines and in isolation from any context, requires the unheard-of power of abstraction traditionally associated with Greek thought. The question "what is philosophy?" is, therefore, also necessarily a question of the turn of the mind that allows one to ask such a question and the methodological discipline that it requires. In short, this question is inevitably a question of philosophy's origin; indeed, the question is inseparable from it. Faced with the question of what they have been doing all their lives, D&G are thus made to look back at the beginning of philosophy in ancient Greece.

This starting point of *What Is Philosophy?*—inquiring into what they have been doing while doing philosophy—clearly stresses that what they have been doing all their lives has been philosophy, even though certain works of theirs, as well as the terminology they have created, seem to suggest otherwise. In *Negotiations,* Deleuze explicitly claims that with *Anti-Oedipus* and, especially, *A Thousand Plateaus,* both he and Guattari sought to create a philosophy, adding that his books on cinema and painting are "philosophy books" as well.[8] This state of affairs will also determine my approach to this late work of theirs.

D&G are certainly not the only thinkers to have asked the question "what is philosophy?" But, as they point out, "the bibliography on the nature of philosophy is very limited" (1). Undoubtedly, there is no philosopher who has not at one point or another responded to that question, but few, indeed, have devoted a full length contribution to it. As the title of their inquiry seems to suggest, Heidegger's essay "Was ist das, die Philosophy?" is one of the few works they have in mind. Notwithstanding the fact that they make no explicit reference to this work, *What Is Philosophy?,* perhaps, seeks to rewrite and replace "Was ist das, die Philosophy?" But any reader who has even the most rudimentary familiarity with philosophy quickly becomes aware that D&G's *What Is Philosophy?* is neither an introduction to philosophical thought nor an attempt to define it within the framework of the philosophical tradition. Their answer to the question "what is philosophy?" does not resonate with many of the handed-down evidences about philosophy. On the contrary, their response to the question of the nature of philosophy amounts to an attempt to put philosophy as it has been practiced throughout the tradition radically into question. Their answer is in a strange way at odds with the history of what has been done in the name of philosophy. But there is another reason why what they show philosophy to be is largely unrecognizable from the point of view of traditional, or academic, philosophy: the question "what is philosophy?"—at least as it is posed in the "Introduction: The question then . . ."—is truly "What is it I have been doing all my life?" (1). *What Is Philosophy?* responds at first, and primarily, to the question of what it is precisely that they have been *doing* while doing philosophy, and, although they have indeed done nothing else but philosophy while doing philosophy, they also have been doing it differently from the way in which professional philosophers do it. With the prime focus of their book being on what they have been doing all their lives in doing philosophy, it is to be expected that their answer to the question "what is philosophy?" distinguishes itself, in both style and content, from earlier responses to it.[9] Yet, what motivates, or even necessitates them to do philosophy, doing it also in a way different from most of the tradition, is something that I will only be able to assess in the process, if not only toward the end, of my reading of this late work.

So far, I have stressed the claim made at the opening of *What Is Philosophy?* that the question pursued in this work is one that can perhaps be posed and answered only late in life when one looks back on what one has been doing as a philosopher. But, in an interview from 1988 given after the completion of his book on the fold in Leibniz, Deleuze also remarks that *The Fold* "leaves [him] in a position [*me rend libre*] . . . to write a book on 'What is philosophy?' "[10] And he adds: "Everything folds, unfolds, enfolds in Leibniz; it's in the folds of things that one perceives, and the world is enfolded in each soul, which unfolds this or that region of it according to the order of space and time . . . The baroque carries folding to infinity." Admittedly, for Deleuze, the fold is a "good philosophical concept" and "a long way from having been exhausted in all its potentialities."[11] Now, if Deleuze is set free to reflect on what philosophy is after having elaborated on a philosophy in which the fold is raised to infinity, then it is because Leibniz's generalization of the fold made such a reflection and questioning possible, in a way, moreover, that is not merely "reflective" and that also breaks with previous attempts to answer that question. As we will later see, for D&G, philosophy is not reflection. If all reflection is always *about* something, and without exception about something that is already fully accomplished, then the problematic of the fold would seem to allow for an application of thought to what D&G have done in the name of philosophy that would not merely reproduce on a higher level what de facto they have done all their lives but would be another way of doing philosophy again and, in the same breath, an opportunity for producing a novel sense of what philosophy is. In other words, although a work that perhaps can be accomplished only late in life, *What Is Philosophy?* is not just a retrospective account of what D&G have been doing all along; it is a work of philosophy in its own right, one that, in addition, intends to produce a novel and unheard-of conception of what philosophy is.

In the same way as Heidegger in "Was is das, die Philosophy?," D&G, so as to reflect on what they have been doing all their lives in doing philosophy, also travel to Greece as the birthplace of philosophy to determine what is so specific about this "Greek miracle," acknowledging in passing that, indeed, they owe the expression to Renan's "celebrated text on the Greek 'miracle'"(224n14). Let me point out right away that if D&G resort to Renan's expression, it is, as we will see, because they subscribe to the idea that what happened in Greece was unique. Even though they embrace this expression, however, this does not prevent them also from distancing themselves from it. Indeed, if at one point they question the pertinence of the term, it is only because, as will become evident, the expression still suggests too strongly that what happened in Greece against all odds was after all inevitable, that is, necessary. In short, the expression is not radical enough to capture what, according to them, happened in Greece.

In what follows, then, I wish to focus on D&G's turn in this late work to the origins of philosophy in Greece. If I do so, however, it is not because I intend to question what is, undoubtedly, a very traditional gesture. After all, as the name itself indicates, philosophy is a Greek thing. Nevertheless, thus singling out D&G's concern with philosophy's Greek origins in *What Is Philosophy?* calls for some preliminary remarks. Indeed, why privilege this question about the birthplace of philosophy in a book that brings up numerous other philosophical topoi and that is about the essence not only of philosophy but also of the sciences and the arts? As I have already indicated, the answer to the question concerning the nature of philosophy makes a return to its origins in Greece inevitable. To understand what is so specific about philosophy in distinction, in particular, from mythical and religious forms of thought, which themselves are not limited to Greece, it is necessary to inquire into the emergence of the main tenets of rational thought in Greek antiquity, and the kind of questions and inquiries that it made possible. This happened, indeed, at one particular moment in time and in one specific part of the world, or the earth, namely, Greece. But what is the relation of philosophy to the place of its birth? Is the locality in which philosophy arises of any importance to it? If philosophy emerges in a determined geographical spot, in what sense does this territorial origin of philosophy affect philosophical thought itself? Does it make the rational and universal thrust of philosophy a merely local thing, as, nowadays, is often believed? Or does philosophy transcend the time and the space of its origin? Although D&G's gesture of retracing philosophy back to its Greek origins has the appearance of an academic and professorial exercise, does it not also represent an effort to rethink the relation of philosophy to territoriality, a relation in which territoriality is neither exterior nor interior to philosophy to the degree of voiding all its claims to universality?

Philosophy as a Greek thing, the authors hold, is a mode of thought thoroughly distinct from other modes, or forms, of thought, such as the arts and the sciences, but this distinction does not imply that philosophy enjoys any particular privilege of its own. Therefore, the following questions impose themselves immediately: what is the status and the role of philosophy in a work that inquires into the essence of this discipline and in which philosophy is lined up with two other disciplines that have equal status? Does philosophy, in spite of its equivalence with the other two forms of thought, not enjoy a certain privilege in that it makes this differentiation of thought conceivable? Now, in *What Is Philosophy?*, the distinction between the three modes of thought in question is made with the help of the terminology and conceptuality of the theory of multiplicities, whose tenets D&G had already systematically exposed and shaped into a systematic tool for the exploration of all kinds of issues, philosophical and nonphilosophical, in *A Thousand Plateaus*. Indeed, since philosophy, as Deleuze contends in *Negotiations*, is a logic of multiplicities,[12] one could argue that, from the start, what D&G have been doing in doing philosophy has been different from the traditional way of philosophizing precisely because they rethought philosophy in terms of the theory of multiplicities, thus giving it a novel means of accounting for itself as a form of thought distinct but also equivalent to other such forms. This philosophical approach to the three forms of multiplicities—philosophy, the arts, and the sciences—seems at first to be at odds with the after all rather traditional, philosophical gesture in *What Is Philosophy?* of harking back to the Greek origins of philosophy. But, in the end, when one looks back with D&G on what they have been doing while doing philosophy, how decisive has this recourse to topological mathematics been for their thought? Rather than an extensive answer to this question, a few hints at how to tackle it must suffice here.

As is evident from *A Thousand Plateaus*, the theory of multiplicities with which D&G are working is, at first, an essentially philosophical theory that they retrace back to Bergson's *Essay on the Immediate Given of Awareness* and Husserl's *Philosophy of Arithmetic*. As D&G observe, the substantive "multiplicity" was created by Bergson in a development parallel to Husserl's elaborations on *Mannigfaltigkeit*, "in order to escape the abstract opposition between the multiple and the one, to cease treating it as a numerical fragment of a lost Unity or Totality or as the organic element of a Unity or Totality yet to come, and instead distinguish between different types of multiplicity."[13] It is this very concern with the classical philosophical problematic of the dualism between the one and the multiple, one that Spinoza, according to Deleuze, approached in a radical form when he elaborated on the relation of substance to its individualizations or modes, that marks D&G's interest in multiplicity. One should not lose sight of this attempt to rethink the venerable philosophical issue of the one and the manifold by way of the concept of multiplicity, particularly, when D&G refer to what they seem to consider the logical and mathematical antecedents, and further technical developments, of the theory of multiplicity. Their frequent references to Bernhard Riemann, Georg Cantor, Alexius Meinong, and Bertrand Russell show that they are speaking more narrowly of set theory and the theory of spaces, but the prime objective they have in putting all these theories to work is still what the theory of multiplicity sought to achieve: to overcome in the name of philosophy the dualism of the one and the manifold, and, in the same breath, the quasi-totality of all philosophy hereto (120–21).[14] And, is the objective not the same as well when in *What Is Philosophy?* they invoke system theory and chaos theory?

Furthermore, before any uncritical celebration of the use of the theory of multiplicities as a radical innovation and the hallmark of D&G's thought, should one not first inquire into the implications of the fact that this theory is presented in *A Thousand Plateaus* by a fictional character who occurs in several novels by Conan Doyle, a pretentious and megalomaniacal figure named Professor Challenger, in an outrageously funny account, moreover, that is written entirely in the grammatical mode of the "imparfait"? Following the exposition of the concept of multiplicity, and Bergson's distinction of two types of multiplicity—one numerical, or extended, and the other qualitative, or intensive—D&G, to overcome the dualism that still haunts this distinction, introduce the professor in question in a chapter entitled "The Geology of Morals." Professor Challenger exposes here the discipline that he pretends to have invented, and which, as his indiscriminate reference to all imaginable disciplines demonstrates, is applicable to both astro- and microphysics. This new discipline, which he refers to by various, and presumably interchangeable names, "the science of multiplicities" being one of them, is a discipline intended to overcome all dualism, and, as regards multiplicity, to demonstrate the intrinsic *assemblage* (*agencement*), or articulation, of its two kinds. Undoubtedly, the unmistakable point of Professor Challenger's lecture, before he exits the scene, his figure literally dissolving and, according to a scenario explicitly attributed to H. P. Lovecraft, pulling the door after him upon entering a coffin-shaped case, is that multiplicity, rather than merely an assemblage of bits and pieces, is intensive, that is, folded upon, and jointed to itself, and in a state of survey in relation to its components.[15] However, does the ludicrous way in which Professor Challenger stages the jumble of the theories he resorts to, including the theory of multiplicity, and the supporting examples, to make this philosophical point, not also reverberate back on their ultimate relevance?

Now, one would perhaps wish to argue that Professor Challenger is a conceptual persona, but as a professor, and with everything D&G offer about professors in *What Is Philosophy?* in mind, one may wonder whether it is not more likely that Professor Challenger is an instance of what D&G diagnose as the "replacement of conceptual personae by teachers or leaders of schools," which they qualify, with Nietzsche (in a sentence that is missing in the English translation), as indicative of the plebs, and a sign of very bad taste in philosophy (80). In any case, the theory of multiplicities in all its logical and mathematical forms is not simply an alternative to philosophy as such, something that could, or would, replace it. In fact, as Deleuze forcefully submits in the "Preface to the English Language Edition" of *Dialogues II,* "set theory and the theory of spaces are still in their infancy."[16] Indeed, it is as if all these theories fell short of what the philosophical theory of multiplicity promised. If notwithstanding their deficiencies all these theories have interested D&G with their focus on multiplicities—such as the multiplicity of forms of thought that are philosophy, the sciences, and the arts—it is, first of all, because they are extensions of empiricism, in other words, of that kind of philosophy that is opposed to transcendental philosophical thought. "Empiricism," Deleuze submits, "is fundamentally linked to a logic—a logic of multiplicities."[17] In short, by having recourse to the theory of multiplicity, to set theory, topology, or chaos theory, D&G in no way suggest that they make philosophy obsolete. Quite the opposite is the case. It is philosophy that drives D&G's interest in these theories.

On several occasions, D&G recognize that philosophy today has numerous competitors that pretend to have done with philosophy, such as the sciences first and foremost but also sociology, psychoanalysis, and Marxism, to name only a few. By contrast, in *What Is Philosophy?* D&G not only mount a highly powerful defense of philosophy's irreducible uniqueness; they argue also that philosophy's competitors do nothing but usurp its position in declaring philosophy dead. Thus, as Deleuze points out in *Dialogues II,* "there is not really much point in wondering whether philosophy is dead, when many other disciplines are assuming its function."[18] In *What Is Philosophy?,* D&G even assert that to claim that philosophy has come to an end, or that metaphysics is to be overcome, "is just tiresome, idle chatter" (9) and that what is done in the name of these claims is after all nothing other than philosophy, or metaphysics. They write: "So long as there is a time and place for creating concepts, the operation that undertakes this will always be called philosophy, or will be indistinguishable from philosophy even if it is called something else" (ibid.). Do these remarks in *What Is Philosophy?* not suggest that to follow up on a classical thread in that work—the Greek origin of philosophy—is not only justified, but also necessary, but that the more traditional approach to philosophy that it presupposes is imperative if one wishes to make any sense of the importance that D&G have given, for example, to such theories as the theory of multiplicity and if, furthermore, one is to evaluate what in fact these theories do for them?

In any event, if, hereafter, I intend to highlight D&G's remarks in *What Is Philosophy?* about the "Greek miracle" and to expand on the geophilosophical essence of philosophy in terms of this miracle, I admittedly pursue an aspect of their thought that is clearly one of the hallmarks of traditional, continental philosophy. Furthermore, what they assert about the specificity of philosophy in general is highly indebted to their analysis of the Greek miracle in question. Yet at the end of the book D&G also hint at a nonphilosophical understanding of philosophy, one which encompasses it and of which philosophy itself is said to be in need. In due time, I will address the issue of how the theory of multiplicity, which serves the authors to articulate the differences and relations among philosophy, the arts, and the sciences, may also be tied in with this broader realm of the negative in which philosophy seems to be inscribed. The expansion of the philosophical to the nonphilosophical, D&G argue, is demanded by philosophy itself, and here again I think that, perhaps, it is the "Greek miracle" that will provide us with some clues of how to conceive such an expansion to begin with.

Before I continue to explore the specific sense in which D&G understand Renan's "Greek miracle," let me first highlight some of the obvious implications of the expression. As the Random House Webster's Unabridged Dictionary tells us, a miracle is "an effect or extraordinary event in the physical world that surpasses all known human or natural powers and is ascribed to a supernatural cause." Any miracle whether performed by men or a divine agent implies the interruption of a causal series of events in whose context it represents something wholly unexpected. Obviously, no supernatural cause is involved in the "Greek miracle," but it is a singular event that is miraculous, as it were, because no causality of any kind seems able to explain it. Although, as Jean-Pierre Vernant, to whom D&G frequently refer, has argued in a sociohistorical approach to the emergence of philosophy in sixth-century Greece, a number of circumstances in ancient Greece, such as the abolishment of the suffocating monarchic presence in the Minoan and Mycenaean civilizations, the ensuing crisis of sovereignty, and the birth of the polis, definitely favored the emergence of the miracle in question, thus casting off "the character of a pure [*absolue*] revelation that scholars have sometimes bestowed upon it."[19] In particular, the birth of the political in the form of *isegoria* (the equal right to speech) and, later, of democracy in Greece undoubtedly favored the appearance of philosophy. But while these developments are not in themselves miraculous, since the political realm and democracy had been prepared well in advance, as Marcel Detienne has shown in *The Masters of Truth in Archaic Greece,* by the assembly of the warriors who, to share out between them the spoils of war, sat around a common place (*meson,* a common point) in which each warrior was seated at equal distance from the center, thus forming the first public space that anticipated the agora in which the citizens entertained relations of perfect reciprocity with one another, they do not allow one to derive philosophy from them in a deterministic fashion.[20] They cannot seamlessly account for the emergence of philosophy in the particular form it took at that precise moment in Greece. In "Remarques," his short response to papers by Eric Alliez and Francis Wolff at a conference organized by Barbara Cassin on "Nos Grecs et leurs modernes," Deleuze suggests that the three fundamental traits of Athenian *autochthony, philia,* and *doxa,* are "perhaps, the conditions for the birth and development of philosophy."[21] Although these traits are of a different kind from the sociohistorical conditions that Vernant evokes, they are still conditions and certainly not causes! Hence, the expression "Greek miracle" is not altogether inappropriate. This miracle, which nothing could have anticipated or predicted, is thus a contingent event, one that could not have happened as well, an event, in short, that occurred without anything having made its occurrence absolutely necessary. Jean Beaufret has put it this way: "philosophy is not an eternal necessity which, from the beginning, has accompanied the sojourn of man on the earth. On the contrary, philosophy is born, and has a country of birth, a cradle."[22] In *What Is Philosophy?,* D&G cite another observation by Beaufret from a posthumously published interview, namely, the remark that (according to Heidegger) "the source is everywhere, undetermined, Chinese as well as Arab and Indian . . . But then there is the Greek episode, the Greeks having had the strange privilege to call the source 'being'" (223–24).[23] Philosophy, then, is an event that occurred for the first time in one particular site and only among the inhabitants of a specific region of the world. If the "Greek miracle" is a miracle, it is all the more extraordinary not only because it cannot be explained in terms of historical causality—indeed, nothing anticipated it or made it a necessary event—but also because it happened in Greece alone and, moreover, only once, according to Renan. And since, as Beaufret has noted, philosophy is called "philosophy" not only in our languages but in all languages, "not only in English or German, in Italian or Spanish, but as well in Russian, Arabic and no doubt Chinese," the link of philosophy to its emergence in Greece—and thus its essentially Greek nature—continues to reverberate whenever and wherever philosophical claims are made.[24] Let us ponder for a moment the implications of conceiving what happened in Greece in this manner, according to which the emergence of philosophy is bound to a geographical area and a specific people. A paradoxical consequence of this origin of philosophy in Greece follows: If nothing necessarily determined its emergence in Greece and among the Greek people, then, rather than being a merely local event, it could, in principle, also have happened somewhere else. Furthermore, could it not, for the same reason, have happened before the "Greek miracle" strictly speaking? Precisely because nothing made it a necessary occurrence, it could, indeed, have happened elsewhere and at an earlier time, as well. But it did not! Although it happened only once and, furthermore, in a specific geographical location but without at all being causally intertwined with the territory in question—hence enjoying the status of an abstraction (one that confers on it the unheard-of power of abstraction characteristic of philosophical thought)—the "Greek miracle" is, for this very reason, capable of being repeated, repetitions that have already occurred in Europe, in particular, but elsewhere, perhaps, as well. From the start, the notion of a "Greek miracle," however unique, implies the possibility (but in no way the necessity) of more miracles, of other miracles to come. What emerged with the Greek miracle—philosophy—then, is something that is also potentially plural.

2

Which Earth?

As we have seen, for Renan, the "Greek miracle" happened only once and will never be seen again, though its effect will last eternally. It is the crystallization in Pentelican marble of the idea of perfection, which for him represents an atemporal standard against which any world, especially our contemporary world, must be measured. Yet, this is certainly not the sense of the "Greek miracle" as D&G understand it. For them, as we will see, philosophy is also an essentially Greek thing in that it emerged solely in that specific region of the world, and if afterward it emerges elsewhere it is in the shape of a creative reinvention of the first beginning. Now, D&G claim that philosophy, this specifically Greek thing, is also by nature geophilosophical. "Geophilosophy" is a concept, according to D&G, that was founded (but not named) by Nietzsche in an effort "to determine the national characteristics of French, English, and German philosophy" (102). Undoubtedly, with this reference to the "national characteristics" of the different European philosophies, D&G's source is chapter 8 of *Beyond Good and Evil,* entitled "Peoples and Fatherlands." If, indeed, Nietzsche's characterization of European philosophies by their national features is said to be the first draft of geophilosophy, then in what sense must this notion be understood? Does it not follow from this concern with the national particularities of French, English, and German philosophies that the term "geophilosophy," which, as Stephan Günzel has argued, D&G "place with Nietzsche into the center of a poststructuralist determination of philosophy,"[1] only suggests that philosophy is geographically anchored and that, hence, it is always something relative as far as its articulations are concerned. Indeed, it seems to me that this is how D&G's claim is sometimes understood. It is true that, by highlighting *autochthony, philia,* and *doxa* as the three traits characteristic of Greek philosophy, Deleuze himself may have contributed to an understanding of the geophilosophical nature of Greek philosophy in such a Nietzschean (and, allegedly, poststructuralist) vein, as a function of a national characteristic that is specifically Greek.[2] But I will show in what follows that the term "geophilosophy" in *What Is Philosophy?* does not at all mean that philosophy is simply geographical in the sense of the physical environment that determines in each case a specific philosophy. Rather, as already pointed out, D&G's claim is not only that philosophy is in essence a Greek thing but also that philosophy as such is in essence geophilosophy. What does that mean?

To answer this question let me first point out that, even if the idea of geophilosophy may have to be retraced to Nietzsche, the term itself is, as far as I know, one that D&G have coined themselves along the lines of what Fernand Braudel, the Annales historian, has called "geohistory" in a methodological reflection in *La Méditerranée et le monde méditerranéen à l'époque de Philippe II*. Although the term "geohistory" evokes the well-established German conception of "geopolitics," it is, Braudel holds, "something other, something at once more historical and broader than a schematized spatial history applied to the present and future situation of states, and which more often than not is already inflected from the beginning in a certain direction." By contrast, geohistory would be an attempt to address human problems as spread out in space and, if possible, charted in the form of a map (*cartographié*), that is, in the form of a "meaningful (*intelligente*) human geography," not only for the present but also for the past, detaching geography from the present and forcing it to "rethink, on the basis of its methods and in its spirit, past realities, and, by the same token, what one could call the becomings of history." The thus double aim of geohistory would be to seek, first, to convince the geographers to pay more attention to time and, second, to convince the historians to worry more about the "formidable permanence" of space and what space supports, engenders, makes possible and thwarts. Braudel sums up his programmatic observations by writing that the aim of such a history would be to turn traditional geography, which is "almost exclusively devoted to the study of state borders and administrative divisions without any concern for the earth itself, the climate, the soil, plants and animals, the kinds of life and labor activities," into "a true retrospective human history."[3] Made especially clear in the first part of Braudel's work, "The Share of the Milieu," the geographical is not simply the setting, or scenery, for action, not simply the backdrop against which human culture develops in opposition to, or at least in distinction from, nature. On the contrary, Braudel's point in *La Méditerranée* is that, rather than a natural environment for human activity the geographical is intimately connected to mental and social structures so as to form the milieu for all historical developments. In short, geohistory, rather than a natural history, is the human history of the earth, a history inextricably intertwined with the earth.

In spite of some occasional ambiguities in *What Is Philosophy?*, geophilosophy, according to D&G, is a philosophy of the earth in a way similar to that in which geohistory is the history of the earth, that is, of the both geographical and mental milieu that liberates the possibilities for all human activities. They write: "Philosophy is a geophilosophy in precisely the same way that history is a geohistory from Braudel's point of view" (95). As a first consequence of understanding geophilosophy to be constitutive of philosophy as such, geophilosophy cannot be a particular philosophy. It is not one type of philosophy, one that, in distinction from other types, would be about the earth. Geophilosophy, for instance, is not an eco-philosophy, that is, a philosophy of the *oikos* as the place, or home, of the human being as a biological being that stands in constant interaction with the environment. Undoubtedly, D&G have not been insensitive to the ongoing destruction of our ecosystems, but in *What Is Philosophy?,* I hold, there are no traces of this concern. Earth, in this work, is especially not the object of the sentimentalizing tendencies of environmentalism. No traces of any kind of ecopastoral approach to the earth is to be found here. In the term "geophilosophy," "geo" refers, on the contrary, to an earth as a milieu that determines philosophy from within, an earth that intrinsically belongs to philosophy, an earth that is the turf of philosophical thought. Such thought, in essence, is not about but of the earth that is its pendant. Now, if philosophy is a Greek thing, as D&G emphasize, then the contention that it is involved with, or in, the earth is more than surprising. Indeed, as everyone knows, Greek philosophy is not about the earth but the cosmos as the meaningfully ordered, purposefully articulated, justly arranged and, hence, beautiful whole of the heavens and the earth, that is, the "world" as, according to the Greeks, it emerged from chaos. Yet, even though philosophy for D&G, however Greek it may be, is not concerned with the cosmos, this does not mean that the latter has no place in D&G's thinking. On the contrary, as we will see at one point, the cosmos is the "correlate" of another form of thought.

In what sense, then, do we have to understand "geo," or "earth," in "geophilosophy"? The full sense of the use that D&G make of the term will only progressively emerge. But, in spite of some conceptual inconsistency in *What Is Philosophy?,* I think that it is safe to exclude from the start certain interpretive options, although the intrinsic reasons that they can and must be excluded will only become obvious later. It is also only in the process of reading D&G's study that I will be capable of refining the distinctions I am about to make. The earth, in D&G's sense, is not the planet or the globe, which are the correlates of an objectifying and referential mode of thought. As a referent of thought, the earth as planet or globe belongs to a form of thought other than philosophy, namely, as we will see, the sciences. Nor is the earth, as I have already said, the world in the sense of the cosmos. The cosmos, I will argue later, is the correlate of the form of thought that is art. Nor is the earth one of the four elements that make up the world or the cosmos.[4] For this very reason it is also not identical with what Heidegger calls the earth that is part of the fourfold, which is a reworked notion of cosmos, and where the earth stands in an orderly and dynamic relation of appropriation and disappropriation to the heavens. However, it is also true that when D&G claim that "the earth is not one element among others but rather brings together all the elements within a single embrace while using one or another of them to deterritorialize territory," one cannot but be reminded of the fourfold and interpret deterritorialization as a form of Heideggerian disappropriation (*Ent-eignung*). Finally, and very importantly, the earth is not Mother Earth, *Ge Meter*, or Gaia, the generating, nurturing and, at the same time, bloodthirsty divinity that the Greeks knew from their myths (and Hesiod's *Theogony*), whom, to quote Maurice Blanchot, a modern such as René Char calls upon "when he addresses the 'shifting earth, horrible, exquisite' "; whom "Hölderlin calls . . . Mother Earth, the earth closed upon its silence, the subterranean earth that withdraws into its shadows"; whom "Rilke speaks to . . . thus: 'Earth, is this not what you want, to be reborn invisible in us?' " and whom "Van Gogh shows . . . to us more forcefully still by saying, 'I am attached to the earth.' "[5] The earth with which Greek philosophy, according to D&G, is concerned is not an already constituted object or thing, such as the cosmos, the planet, an element, or the mythical figure Mother Earth.[6] Following up on a remark from *Dialogues II,* I would hold that all these "fixed powers which try to hold us back, the established powers of the earth," must be betrayed (betrayal being a good thing for Deleuze) to creatively construct the earth that is the very issue of philosophy.[7] The earth with which philosophy from early Greece on is concerned is both intrinsic to philosophy as philosophy and at the same time something that, rather than being given in advance, needs to be constructed. If D&G's philosophy, as some have held, is one that brings philosophy down to earth, it is paradoxically earth as we do not know it. And this is the case in several senses that we will have to clarify. Indeed, let us keep in mind that in *What Is Philosophy?* the earth, *la terre,* is characterized as the deterritorialized par excellence, in other words, as an earth liberated from any particular territory, that of the earth included, in short, as a highly abstract earth, as it were.[8] Let me also point out that, according to *Negotiations,* the earth as the deterritorialized is "something deeper" than any territory.[9] The earth, we are told, is that of the philosopher; it is the ground on which he philosophizes. Yet, if philosophy comes into being in Greece as geophilosophy by nature, it is also because from the start something that concerns the earth—in D&G's terms, the deterritorialized par excellence—is nonetheless immediately reterritorialized onto a particular part of the earth, onto the earth of the Greeks, their world, the world that for them is this world. However, this is in no way to suggest that philosophy is merely a Greek phenomenon without significance for the rest of the world. On the contrary, it is something that concerns the earth as such, but always in the complementary form of a reterritorialization. This inevitable reterritorialization of the deterritorialized earth is what makes philosophy in essence necessarily singular, and that means also potentially plural. The "Greek miracle," then, is no longer of the order of an atemporal standard, as was still the case with Renan, but the event of the emergence of a concern with the earth as such in an always singular fashion.

We thus need to get a more precise grasp of what territory and earth mean and how their relationship is to be understood if, according to D&G, the latter is the interstice in which philosophical thought occurs. To do this, it will be imperative to clarify the double movement of deterritorialization and reterritorialization. But first a remark on D&G's terminology. In *Dialogues II,* Deleuze holds that "there are no literal words, [and] neither are there metaphors (all metaphors are sullied words, or else make them so). There are only inexact words to designate something exactly." Hence the need to "create extraordinary words, on condition that they be put to the most ordinary use and that the entity they designate be made to exist in the same way as the most common object."[10] A little later, Deleuze makes the following remark about the terminology that both he and Guattari have used: "In none of the cases are we making a metaphorical use of it: we don't say that is 'like.' . . . We are using deterritorialized terms, that is, terms which are torn from their area, in order to reterritorialize another notion."[11] What Deleuze advances here about his and D&G's terminology would at first seem to thwart the methodological concern of my reading of *What Is Philosophy?,* namely, retranslating their terminology back into more common philosophical language. Indeed, if there are no literal meanings of terms that could lend themselves to their metaphorologization, it would seem to be impossible to return to a term's literal meaning. Yet, the conception of language on the basis of which Deleuze makes his remarks on literal meaning and metaphor also implies that all terms of language are always already translated terms—terms that have been detached from previous signifiers and contexts—and have always already been applied in different contexts to different objects. Language is, thus, construed as a medium of translation; each of its words is a translated word, torn from a previous area, and applied to another area, each translation being a creative act: the creation of an extraordinary word. But if this is the case, a trace of, and reference to, the meaning and context from which a word is lifted, that is, deterritorialized, and subsequently reterritorialized on another notion, remains in each newly created term which not only justifies its retranslation into its previous term, but ultimately requires it to be understood in its novelty. In short, rather than putting my methodological approach in question, Deleuze's remarks on words as lacking literal meaning legitimatize it.

In addition, what Deleuze says here about the way he and D&G use common terms, transforming them in such a way as to become extraordinary terms, is of considerable help in clarifying the way they understand the terms *deterritorialization* and *reterritorialization* themselves, especially since these terms, as one can see here, are employed in significantly differing, problematic contexts. Yet, although the terms in question are regularly used in ways in which their literal meanings may only play at best a secondary role, it is precisely this literal meaning, that is, the reference to "earth" (*la terre*) in "territory," "deterritorialization," and "reterritorialization," that is decisive in *What Is Philosophy?*[12] It is in this work, therefore, that what the movements of deterritorialization and reterritorialization accomplish with respect to a territory, and, finally, to the earth itself, is at issue and becomes the point of departure for a clarification of these terms in the first place.

The expression "line of flight," which originates with the arts and refers to the vanishing point in perspectival representations, can serve as our starting point here.[13] Deleuze reinterprets this expression by placing the emphasis on "flight" and makes fleeing (and betrayal) a positive, creative activity. He thus can define deterritorialization as consisting in a "line of flight," that is, in the creative evasion or simply the departure from a territory in all its self-enclosedness and the opening toward an outside, or other, as a result of which one betrays and turns away from "the fixed powers which try to hold us back, the established powers of the earth."[14] In other words, deterritorialization consists in tracing a line of abstraction that, ultimately, has "an extreme of abstraction" in which the earth is liberated from all its established determinations as its goal.[15] Now, since there are all sorts of territories to leave and from which to abstract, there are as many senses of deterritorialization in D&G. But, obviously, the territory to which deterritorialization refers at first is that of *terra, terre,* that is, the earth itself. After having evoked several ways in which to speak of deterritorialization, Deleuze remarks that, "at the limit, it is the Earth itself, the deterritorialized," that is meant.[16] Even though D&G do not explicitly acknowledge it, that which is left behind and escaped, namely, the earth in all its established powers, leaves an inevitable trace in the deterritorialized territory. Indeed, the term "deterritorialization" itself implies the tearing away in abstraction from the earth only to create what D&G call the earth as the deterritorialized par excellence, in other words, an abstract earth, if not the earth as the abstraction par excellence, before all subsequent reterritorialization or application onto a particular territory (or earth again, as we will see). Moreover, since the earth is the place of dwelling shared by all, the term deterritorialization continues to resonate with the meaning of "universality," "generality," or "ideality."[17] In short, what both thinkers of radical immanence, that is, of an immanence that refuses any compromise with transcendence, call the earth stands in a relation to territory that is not unlike that of the universal to the particular, even though the earth is not simply the universal as we know it, and territory not simply the particular. When D&G remark that "the earth constantly carries out a movement of deterritorialization on the spot, by which it goes beyond any territory: it is deterritorializing and deterritorialized" (85), the point is that the earth de-particularizes on the spot any territory and raises it to the level of generality, or universality. These movements of deterritorialization and reterritorialization are essentially, then, the complementary movements of operations of clearing a ground and of laying a foundation. But, as we noticed already, such a deterritorializing universalization is also, in turn, immediately reterritorialized, that is, reinscribed onto a part of the earth in the form of a territory.

To make these notions and their corresponding movements more precise, I circle back to some of the relevant passages in which D&G explicitly address the earth's movement as one of deterritorialization. Now, to accomplish this I must anticipate certain issues that I can develop in detail only later. Anyone who is familiar with *What Is Philosophy?* knows that for D&G philosophy, distinct from the sciences and the arts, consists in the creation of concepts. Philosophy is the creation of concepts, however, not in the thin air of abstraction but on a plane of immanence, that is, on the plane that is "instituted" by the nonphilosophical and prephilosophical intuition of a "One-All" (which I will argue later translates the Greek expression *hen kai pan*) that cuts through chaos and that, subsequently, is populated by these concepts.[18] Since this pre-philosophical and still conceptual plane is a presupposition of philosophy as the creation of concepts, it is an internal and intrinsic condition of philosophy (41). Indeed, as such an internal condition of philosophy, as something that is required for concept creation, the nonconceptual plane of immanence is something that is instituted by philosophy itself. D&G make this point rather forcefully when they hold that "prephilosophical does not mean something preexistent but rather something *that does not exist outside philosophy,* although philosophy presupposes it. These are its internal conditions. The nonphilosophical is perhaps closer to the heart of philosophy than philosophy itself" (41). Now, D&G claim that this plane of the One-All "constitutes the absolute ground of philosophy, its earth [*sa Terre*] or deterritorialization, the foundation on which it creates its concepts. Both the creation of concepts and the instituting of the plane are required, like two wings or fins" (41). Our authors could not be more clear: the earth with which philosophy is involved is the plane of immanence, in short, the intuited unity of all that is and with respect to which it creates its concepts. Within philosophy, then, the earth is philosophy's inherent and absolute ground, presupposed by it insofar as philosophy is the creation of concepts, but a ground that philosophy itself institutes as its own nonphilosophical foundation and that, rather than transcendent, is thus thoroughly immanent to philosophy itself. By instituting earth as its absolute ground, philosophy is fundamentally geophilosophy, which means not only, as now becomes clear, that philosophy is borne by the earth but also that it is a thoroughly autonomous construction because its ground, its earth, is entirely immanent to it. If the earth that belongs to philosophy (*sa Terre*), and subtends philosophical concept-creation is a deterritorialization, that is, Earth with a capital E, the Earth in an absolute sense and free from all the particularities of a territory, then the Earth is, in traditional philosophical language, philosophy's universal ground. And the concepts that it creates, which come to populate the ground that holds it up from within, are the inevitable means of fleshing out this fully immanent ground. Furthermore, it should draw our attention that, by deterritorializing territories and thus instituting the earth as its absolute foundation, philosophy accomplishes a self-referentiality specifically its own, independent of any particularities of territories. In this context, the question posed at the end of the first paragraph of Chapter 4 of *What Is Philosophy?,* entitled "Geophilosophy," is particularly significant. D&G ask: "In what sense . . . is Greece the philosopher's territory or philosophy's earth?" (86). Simplifying a bit, the response to this question is that Greece is the earth of philosophy in the sense that the conception was born of an earth and an existence that are self-foundational, autonomous, free from all attachment to particular territories, born, in short, of a fully immanent earth whose internal consistency is not diminished by the existence of an outside cause or reason. In an earlier passage in *What Is Philosophy?* concerning the necessity to distinguish between conceptual personae and psychosocial types (the latter referring to Georg Simmel and Erving Gofman), the authors inquire into "the formation of territories, the vectors of deterritorialization, and the process of reterritorialization" (68). It is in this context that the complementarity of the movements of deterritorialization and reterritorialization is mentioned for the first time. The earth, as we have seen, is the result of a movement of liberation from territories; it is the deterritorialized as such, but, at the same time that such deterritorialization occurs, the earth (as the absolute and universal ground of philosophy) is reterritorialized again onto Greece, that is, onto a territory (and a historical culture) that itself is no longer a natural given but presupposes a prior deterritorialization.[19] D&G remark that "if we are looking for the originality of the Greek world we must ask what sort of territory is instituted by the Greeks, how they deterritorialize themselves, on what they are reterritorialized" (ibid.). Let me point out right away that in what follows, then, we will have to distinguish between two interrelated forms of earth. There is, on the one hand, the Earth as the absolute ground of philosophy, the deterritorialized world par excellence, and, on the other, an earth that is historically instituted, such as the earth or world fashioned by the Greeks, and on which the philosopher reterritorializes the Earth in a philosophical sense. The relation between both will occupy us in detail later.

Geophilosophy is philosophy as concerned not only with the Earth (the universal world) but also with the particular territory on which the Earth becomes reterritorialized, in which it becomes incarnated, if I may dare say so. This particular territory is, as will become evident later, not a natural or physical but a primarily political territory made up of the specifically Greek organizational characteristics of society (freedom, democracy) and the specifically Greek psychosocial types (the friend, the rival). Let us recall that, at the beginning of the chapter on "Geophilosophy," D&G asked: "In what sense . . . is Greece the philosopher's territory or philosophy's earth?" Undoubtedly, it is in the sense that Greece is a territory that is restored, or given back, again by the Earth as the result of its reterritorialization and in the sense that this restored territory, rather than an original or natural territory, is a thoroughly transformed one not only insofar as it contains specifically Greek institutions and specifically Greek types—"(the Friend, for example?)"—but also, significantly enough, insofar as it "open[s] onto an elsewhere" (86).[20] By being both deterritorializing and reterritorializing, the Earth "goes beyond any territory . . . It merges with the movement of those who leave their territory en masse, with crayfish that set off walking in file at the bottom of the water, with pilgrims or knights who ride a celestial line of flight" (85).[21] By going beyond any territory, the Earth of philosophy, but also, as we will see, the earth as a territory through reterritorialization, rather than being enclosed spaces, open upon an elsewhere through migration and let themselves be exposed to others.

3

An Autochthonous No Longer Earthbound

Let me circle back to D&G's question from the chapter on "Geophilosophy," namely, "in what sense . . . [Greece is] the philosopher's territory or philosophy's earth" (86). To respond to this question, I will have to take on more directly the topic of the "Greek miracle." In preparation, I wish to preface my commentary by another brief digression on Renan's "Prière sur l'Acropole." Addressing the goddess Athena, Renan proclaims that "the world will only be saved when the world returns to her, and repudiates its barbarous bonds." Renan then declaims:

> Firmly believing in you, I will resist my fatal counselors: my skepticism, which causes me to have doubts about the people; my spiritual restlessness, which, once truth has been discovered, incites me to continue searching; my fantasy, which after reason has spoken, hinders me to stay at rest. O Archegetes, the ideal that the man of genius incarnates in his works of art, I prefer being the least important in your house rather than the first elsewhere . . . I will become the servant of the last of your sons. The current inhabitants of the earth which you gave to Erechtheus, I will exalt them, I will flatter them . . .[1]

It will eventually become clear that Archegetes, or Apollo Archegetes, is a crucial figure in understanding why, according to D&G, Greece is the philosopher's territory or philosophy's earth.

First, however, a number of steps are necessary. In a line of thought that is more historical, sociological, and psychosocial than philosophical and that thus concerns the earth as it comes into being in Greek civilization, D&G state that it is not correct to conceive, as is often the case, the Greek states and city-states as territorial entities that would have arisen by way of a substitution of "a territorial principle for the principle of lineage" (86). On the contrary, state and city are based on a deterritorialization. Polis is usually translated in French as "cité"; in German or English it is usually translated as city-state. However, D&G clearly distinguish the two aspects of the polis when they write that:

> State and City . . . carry out a deterritorialization because the former juxtaposes and compares agricultural territories by relating them to a higher arithmetical Unity, and the latter adapts the territory to a geometrical extensiveness that can be continued in commercial circuits. The *imperial spatium* of the State and the *political extensio* of the city are not so much forms of a territorial principle as a deterritorialization that takes place on the spot [*sur le vif*] when the State appropriates the territory of local groups or when the city turns its back on its hinterland. In one case, there is reterritorialization on the palace and its supplies; and in the other, on the agora and commercial networks. (Ibid.)

In what follows, I will first pursue what D&G establish with regard to the polis as city. What our authors assert here about the formation of a civic space in Greece seems to refer to what scholars have characterized as Cleisthenes's "largely revolutionary" reform, if not " 'reconstitution' [*Neugründung*]," of the Greek polis toward the end of the fifth century.[2] Nicole Loraux, for her part, characterizes this reform inaugurated by Cleisthenes as an "essential interruption in Athenian temporality."[3] D&G's characterization of the formation of the civic space of the polis in terms of "a geometrical . . . *political extensio* of the city" as opposed to the "higher arithmetical Unity" of the state seems to refer to the contention by some scholars that Cleisthenes's reform was of "an exceptional maturity in which abstraction dominated pragmatism since one senses in this reform the influence of the philosophical and arithmetical systems developed by the Ionian philosophers (one has spoken about 'decimal democracy')."[4] I do not need to evoke here the special circumstances that led to Cleisthenes's initiative, nor what the much discussed political motives for this reform by an aristocrat may have been. Suffice it to say that through his reform he freed the city from the vicissitudes of the stasis between the noble families (whose strife for power in archaic Greece represented at that time the essence of "political" life) by having recourse to the *demos,* the people, and thus gave Athens a rule of freedom that later was to evolve into what became known as "democracy." As a result of this interruption, Athens, as it is generally acknowledged, enjoyed two hundred years of democratic life.

Now, what exactly comprised this reform, which resulted in the practical realization of *isonomia,* or, literally, the equal participation of the citizens in the polis in the form of *isegoria,* that is, the equal right to speech in all the institutions of the polis?[5] The reform, indeed, consisted in a territorial reorganization of Attica on the basis of demes (*demoi*), that is, the smallest local unities of settlements such as townships that were given a political organization and that cut, as it were, through the old order of the *phylai* (tribes), *gene* (clans), *phratriai* (brotherhoods), and *thiasoi* (cult communities). These demes in turn were used to completely reconstitute and regroup the *phylai* such that they no longer represented particular, local interests. As a result of this reorganization, the civic body of Attica completely changed, now detached from the local solidarities that until then had cemented the regional factions. Not only did this reform lead to a new kind of identity of the citizen, one based on political affiliation alone, on the citizen's belonging to the polis that for the first time gave the citizen a civic presence in the city-state, but, as a consequence of the reorganization of the tribes and the admission of new citizens, such as nonnatives, freed slaves, and foreigners, the reform also brought about a mixing of citizens, one of its most striking aspects. With this, the one capacity in which all were equal gained supreme importance.[6] As Christian Meier writes: "The members of each phyle were to have nothing in common but their shared citizenship, which was to be the basis of their solidarity."[7]

Rather than installing a territorial principle as the foundation of citizenship and Athenian political life, Cleisthenes, in Loraux's words, "constituted the male citizen-soldiers [*andres*], who already lived in a same place, into organic groups, who, thanks to their residency, enjoyed from there on both a collective solidarity and a personal identity."[8] Now, according to Loraux—and with this we return to the problematic of *What Is Philosophy?*—this creation of a civic space in Athens took place "at the price of what has been called a 'de-spatialization,' and which, for her part, [as she says], she would rather call a deterritorialization."[9] Following Aristotle's distinction in *Athenaion Politeia* between *khora* (understood here in its still pre-philosophical sense as civic space, a definite geographical space isolated by borders from the outside) and *topos* (place), Loraux argues that at the very moment the eminent quality of being an Athenian, and, hence, a citizen, devolved from the fact of being linked by the reciprocity of those who belonged to a deme, that is, to an institution in which the grouping of its inhabitants and their reciprocal relations prevailed over its spatial dimension, *khora* progressively made room for topos.[10] She concludes: "If *topos* [as Aristotle says in *Physics*] is 'the primal envelope of that of which it is the topos,' it is no longer the territory [*khora*], but the demes which contain—and only contain—the population of the demotes." As a consequence, "the Attic earth is dismissed as regards its pretensions to entertain an intimate relation to the citizens."[11] To return, then, to D&G's question concerning the "sense" in which Greece is "the philosopher's territory or philosophy's earth," it should be clear that for D&G the earth in question can no longer be Gé, or Gaia, no longer, in Hesiod's words, the "wide-bosomed Earth, the ever-sure foundation of all" in reference to which the Attic people consistently made their claim for autochthony, for having been born from the earth.[12]

Apart from the fact that it is incorrect to define the Greek states and cities as territories, D&G hold that the deterritorialization by which alone they are constituted has in each of them a different shape. Commonly referred to as city-states, D&G, as we have seen already, consider the poleis on the basis of their functions as (imperial) States *and* (democratic) Cities, that is, as cities, and cities as centers of states. They write that the deterritorialization in States "tends to develop vertically from on high, according to a celestial component of the earth." It "takes place through transcendence." As a result, "the territory has become desert earth, but a celestial Stranger arrives to reestablish the territory or reterritorialize the earth. In the city, by contrast, deterritorialization takes place through immanence: it frees [*libère*] an Autochthon ["the Autochthon citizen"], that is to say, a power of the earth that follows a maritime component that goes under the sea to reestablish the territory (the Erechtheum, temple of Athena and Poseidon)" (86).[13] Before I make the first of several attempts at clarifying this rather elliptic, if not seemingly counterintuitive, passage—proceeding in the manner of a detective, not unlike, perhaps, a character in a Conan Doyle story, until, finally, I will be able to address the reason for its obscurity and to establish what is meant by it—let me point out that the deterritorialized territory of the city is that of a "*milieu of immanence*" (87) in which the Autochthon is set free, or, more specifically, in which the autochthonous citizen is liberated from one kind of autochthony and given another, a free autochthony. Spelling "Autochthon" with a capital *A* is a clear indication that it must be taken in a higher sense than what the term usually denotes, which is further supported by the fact that such an Autochthon is said to be set free by the milieu of immanence that characterizes the polis. As we have seen, *autochthony, philia,* and *doxa* are the three specifically Greek traits. If D&G translate these features here as "immanence, friendship, and opinion" (88), there can be no doubt that the autochthony they are speaking about must be thought as, or from, immanence. Immanence stands in opposition to transcendence. That a certain conception of autochthony could be linked to immanence is suggested already by Kant, who, in the context of a discussion of the ideas of reason in *Critique of Pure Reason,* for example, defines immanence as "indigenous (*einheimisch*)," as native, or local, rather than transcending the territory.[14] But, needless to say, considering the ideological implications of the concept of autochthony, the definitely positive use that D&G seem to make of this notion is startling.

Now, the maritime component of the earth mentioned in the passage cited above, and by way of which autochthony is, unmistakably, linked to the opposite of the land, that is, to the sea, seems to refer to Poseidon who, according to Athens's foundational myth as it has been recounted by Apollodores and Saint Augustine, was first to arrive in Attica, causing water (the *Erechtheis*) to burst forth from a hole on the Acropolis. Although the olive tree only appeared there subsequently upon the orders of Athena,[15] the citizens settled the difference between the two gods vying for patronage over the site in favor of Athena, whose name became that of the city while Poseidon went underground, or rather undersea, as the passage seems to intimate.[16] I will return in due time to Poseidon's place in the Erechtheum. In any event, D&G immediately point out that the difference between the two forms of deterritorialization involved in the formation of the state and the city respectively is in fact a bit more complicated, since "the imperial Stranger," who can be no other than Apollo Archegetes, "himself needs surviving autochthons . . . and the citizen Autochthon [for his part] calls on strangers in flight," that is, strangers fleeing imperial Asia (86; trans. mod.). But the surviving "autochthons" (which, in the original French text, is not capitalized as is, on the contrary, the "Autochthon" freed by the city) that the imperial Stranger needs are not the same psychosocial types as the Autochthon liberated through immanence by the City. For the time being, however, I will concentrate on the autochthonous citizens liberated by the cities, rather than on those that make up the imperial and colonializing states.

At this juncture a clarification of the notion of autochthony is certainly warranted. As Nicole Loraux has shown in *The Invention of Athens: The Funeral Oration in the Classical City,* autochthony has been an obsession with the Greeks, especially with the Athenians, who seemed to have given themselves over to the delights of narcissism, producing an extensive discourse on autochthony, that is, on the Athenian citizen as having been born from the earth and remaining as such identical to himself, always excelling in his virtues both in his verbal and practical acts.[17] Composed of the pronominal adjective *auto* (self, which as a prefix can mean of or by oneself, independent from) and *khthon* (earth, land, ground), "autochthonous" means sprung from the earth, indigenous, or native (as opposed to settlers).[18] An autochthon is thus an aboriginal, original, or indigenous inhabitant, a native of the land itself. It is in this sense that the original inhabitants of Greece, before the Indo-Germanic migrations that brought the first hellenophone populations, the so-called Proto-Greeks, to the peninsula at the end of the third millennium, could have been called autochthonous. However, it is the Greeks, who came well after them, who coined the epithet not only for themselves but also for their cities, which, unlike Roman cities, were fiercely reserved. Now, even though D&G invoke, in "Example 8" of "Geophilosophy," the plane of immanence as the ground that the Greeks "possessed Autochthonously" (104), their claim that in the polis a deterritorialization of the territory takes place through immanence that "frees an Autochthon, that is to say, a power of the earth that follows a maritime component that goes under the sea to reestablish the territory (the Erechtheum, temple of Athena and Poseidon)," seems to point to a different conception of autochthony and earth than simply the nativeness suggested by the myth of autochthony. A more extensive clarification than the one suggested so far concerning how D&G conceive autochthony is thus warranted if we want to understand what they mean by earth and, mutatis mutandis, Greek philosophy as a philosophy of the earth. However, such a clarification cannot be provided in a simple and unambiguous fashion; it requires several twists and detours.

Before attempting to define this other conception of autochthony at which D&G definitely aim, and, in the same breath, the different sense of earth that it entails, I interrupt my commentary to elaborate briefly on what Plato characterized in the *Republic* as an "opportune falsehood," namely, the Greek conception of autochthony and the fascination with self-referentiality that it entails. According to the official discourse of the city, the Athenians belonged to the land from the beginning, having been born of the earth itself. Yet, if, according to Socrates, the "story" (*mythos*) to be told to the rulers and guardians in the perfect state outlined in the dialogue consists in telling them that they only dreamed that they have been educated and trained for their task, while in reality "they were down within the earth being molded and fostered themselves," it is obvious that autochthony is itself of the order of a myth. Furthermore, when Socrates adds that "when they were quite finished the earth as being their mother delivered them, and now as if their land were their mother and their nurse they ought to take thought for her and defend her against any attack and regard the other citizens as their brothers and children of the selfsame earth," it is perfectly obvious that Plato considers the myth of autochthony an inevitable political ideology required, on the one hand, to justify hierarchy in the state, and, on the other, to secure that "all . . . in the city are brothers."[19] Recognized as a political myth and a lie necessary to secure the cohesion of the state, autochthony in the *Republic* is the object of a first demythologization, a first independent and "enlightened" treatment. Now, to further elaborate on the myth of autochthony I turn to Nicole Loraux's studies on this notion, particularly in *The Children of Athena: Athenian Ideas about Citizenship and the Divi-*

sion between the Sexes. In this work on the Athenian myth of autochthony, on one of the major topoi, in short, that constituted Athenian civic discourse and by means of which Athens reflected its own singular status as a city-state, Loraux shows how Athens legitimated its hegemony over the other poleis and defined what it meant to be a citizen by claiming to be the only people that never emigrated.[20] Thoroughly different from the Roman territorial definition of citizenship, the Athenians equated citizenship with birth, that is, with having been born Athenian. But, as Loraux has shown, even though the polis defines its citizens by their autochthony, that is, as having been born from the soil of the homeland itself, this definition of citizenship took the form of two distinct, even contradictory, but also simultaneous and complementary conceptions of autochthony that coexisted in the city: on the one hand, a mythical autochthony and, on the other, a more laicized or political conception of autochthony.[21] It is for having pointed out this double nature of the conception of autochthony in Greece that I single out Loraux's study, since it may allow us to glean the one Greek conception of autochthony to which D&G are attracted at the expense of the other.

Autochthony either has been bequeathed on the Athenians by a male ancestor who was born from the earth, or it has been accorded to all Athenians collectively in a mythical past, which was later codified by the Periclean Law, insofar as they have been born on Greek soil from both a mother and a father.[22] According to the first model, to be born an Athenian means to be *aner* (a man), which emphasizes the origin of autochthony in an immemorial event in which the first Athenian was born from the earth itself (and, as Loraux points out, without the intervention of any woman); according to the second model, by contrast, it means to have been born from two, a mother and a father, which stresses the collective autochthony of the Athenians and the foundation of their political equality.

Even though there is a child of the Attic soil anterior to Erechtheus, namely the legendary king of Athens called Cecrops, still half human and half serpent, who established the rudiments of civilization, instituted both monogamy among men and the burial of the dead, and is credited with the invention of writing, I begin with the myth of Erechtheus who, according to Loraux, is the central figure of the first version of the civic myth of autochthony.[23] According to the story, as Hephaestus is in amorous pursuit of the virgin goddess Athena—of Athena Parthenos—he spills his semen on the legs of the fleeing virgin. Brushed off by the goddess, the semen drops on the earth and fertilizes it. Thus, Erechtheus is born as the son of *Gé métér,* the Earth. Athena, daughter of Zeus, picks him up from earth, rears him, and installs him as King of

Athens in the palace of the Acropolis, which he shares with her (that is, with Athena Poliades). Born from the earth, if not even of himself, as it were—neither Gé nor Athena are really mothers to him, nor is Hephaestus truly a father—Erechtheus is the first autochthonous, though also divine, offspring, the first who enjoys a "goodness of birth (*eugeneia*)," and as such he is the ancestor of all Athenians. This myth of the legendary king provides the model of filial descent of all Athenian men insofar as they are of the land.

In the second version of autochthony, which is purely political, the City itself is the central figure. According to this scenario, which dominates the *epitaphioi,* or funeral oratories, the Athenians are, in Loraux's words, "born from the *political* earth."[24] Whereas the first version states that the Athenians' autochthony is the result of one Autochthon who is a son of the Earth, the second model attributes collective autochthony to all Athenians, who, as *andres athenaioi,* that is, valiant soldier-citizens, are ready to give their lives for the democratic city. Loraux writes that "as the founding topos of discourse about the city, autochthony tells the Athenian citizens that the city is its own origin, its own principle. The city is immemorial [and timeless, RG]."[25] It has always been in the same location and was from the beginning a political entity. According to this model (which is not a filial one and does not instate a lineage), democracy is grafted onto autochthony. The latter is "incorporated by Athenians into the permanent occupation of Attic soil: the Athenians are thus the only legitimate inhabitants, opposed to all those who are so-called immigrants and foreigners, although they are in fact on their own land—that is, all the citizens of other poleis."[26] In distinction from the mythical account of the Athenians' autochthony in which the first Athenian is the offspring of the Earth (and two divinities), the second version stresses the human origin of the city's citizens since only one who has been born from two Athenian parents on a soil that the Athenians have occupied since immemorial time is autochthonous, forming a city that from the beginning is political; the citizens are the result of sexual intercourse and are thus born from the children of the homeland.[27] As already said, these two different discourses on autochthony, however exclusive they may be in positing birth from the Earth or from human parents, are simultaneously present in the civic discourse on the origin of Athenian citizenship.[28]

Now the point I want to make is that D&G's attempt to think autochthony in a way that differs from that of the myth of being born from the Earth for which the story of Erechtheus is the paradigm, which offers a model of filial descent, seems to be closer to the second, political version of the myth of autochthony. But even in this more democratic version of the myth, there is a lot left to be desired.[29] Therefore, we may want to attempt to make a new start, keeping in mind that D&G not only approach the question of autochthony from a philosophical perspective but also frame it with the question "what is philosophy?"; in other words, D&G are intent on showing that autochthony is intrinsically linked up with philosophy as a Greek thing. This approach requires them to depart altogether from the double nature of the civic myth that informs the polis's official reflection on itself.[30] To make this point I will, at this juncture, pursue the question of autochthony and the kind of earth it involves by following a slightly different thread in *What Is Philosophy?* As is well known, to be autochthonous has been for the Greek immigrants a question of great pride. This is particularly so in the case of the Athenians, who also had a foreign origin, although unlike all the other Greeks they claimed to have always occupied the same soil.[31] The Athenians, who contended that they are of the land (especially as opposed to those who came to Greece during the Doric migration), not only became oblivious to their Indo-Germanic origin, but also, as Praxithea shows in a passage from a lost drama from Euripides entitled *Erechtheus,* they, in particular the Athenian women, also confirmed their belonging to the Attic earth by eagerly shedding the blood of their own flesh and offering it to the thirsty Earth whenever the city was in need. As Marcel Detienne and Giulia Sissa have noted in *The Daily Life of the Greek Gods,* in a chapter to which D&G explicitly refer,

> As it winds its way up from the Ceramicus, through the Agora, toward the Acropolis, Autochthony is declined in the political, masculine case. Only males, leaping to her defense, die for the Mother-Country. Fortunately, however, Euripides surprised everyone by setting on the tragic scene a feminine version of Athenian autochthony: an autochthony for women, based on the strength of women, which reexplored the whole mythology of the origins of Athens. Inevitably, all this was spurned by the Bossuet of the national funerals and those who spoke for the undertakers' profession.[32]

The story highlighted by Sissa and Detienne is that of Praxithea, Erechtheus's wife, hence queen of Athens, and as her name suggests the right hand of Athena Poliades. She is the executioner of what is expected of the priestess of the Poliadic cult, who, all by herself and in no way as a mouthpiece for her husband, the king, sacrifices one of her daughters, Chktonia, thus showing "Erechtheus, and everyone, all the assembled citizens, how an autochthonous woman behaved, how an autochthonous mother could shed the blood of her own flesh, in order to offer it to the Earth that is thirsty for it."[33] Shared by both men and women of ancient Greece, the myth of autochthony, if it has to have a philosophical dimension, will thus need to be reconsidered.

Now, as Marcel Detienne reminds us, "the Earth alone is truly autochthonous, [although she also] tolerates the germinal thrust of One-born-from-the-ground-itself."[34] By considering themselves autochthonous the Athenians sought to emulate the autochthony of the Earth itself, yet, as far as human beings are concerned, autochthony is not simply given to them, contrary to what the Athenians proclaimed for themselves. For humans, autochthony is something that takes time to produce. Sissa and Detienne have forcefully argued this point in *The Daily Life of the Greek Gods,* claiming that "autochthony was something that took some time to establish, over several generations."[35] Autochthony is thus a process, and, in conformity with it, the Greeks developed procedures to deterritorialize the Earth, *Gé métér,* as the sole power of autochthony, which tolerated nativeness only as long as it came with the regular sacrifice of the blood of those who always already belonged to the Earth, like Praxithea's daughter Chktonia, or like Aglouros, another female autochthon, who sacrificed herself for the good of the city by jumping from its wall to her death. Undoubtedly, D&G have in mind this meaning of autochthony as something made, rather than something that the Athenians possessed naturally. To clarify a bit the rather difficult passage in which they speak of the Autochthon, I follow up on a footnote that once more refers the reader to Detienne's work, specifically to "Qu'est-ce qu'un site?," an essay that serves as Detienne's introduction to a volume he edited, *Tracés de Fondation,* and that interestingly enough proposes a reflection on rituals and processes "that concern territorialization beyond and even in advance of the act of foundation."[36] Detienne even uses in this context the term "deterritorialization" (in quotation marks), an affirmative nod no doubt to D&G. But the piece that obviously serves as the background for D&G's discussion of autochthony, although they do not explicitly refer to it, is another essay by Detienne in this very volume, an essay entitled "Apollon Archégète: Un modèle politique de la territorialisation."[37] With this reference I also shift the focus away from the polis as City to the polis and the *poleis* as States. Detienne opens the essay in question with the following words: "There is an art of founding oneself, and certain Greeks knew how to raise it to a high level of perfection. If it is true, indeed, that most of the ancient peoples understood themselves as autochthonous by nature, most of them remained simple aboriginals, and this because, undoubtedly, they thought that the idea of foundation should remain foreign to the one of autochthony. From very early on, the citizens of Athens have made a choice" to "give birth to themselves, and this without end."[38] Detienne continues, "at least since Hesiod's cosmogony, the Earth possesses the power of the Self to engender the Other." Yet, this does not mean that the autochthonous Earth, Gaia, is simply driven "to found in all its alterity." Rather, this is what the Greeks took upon themselves, replacing natural autochthony with an entirely different one, one that is other than natural autochthony, an autochthony created through self-foundation on the basis of political freedom alone. Detienne writes: "The originality of the Greeks—in all comparative simplicity—was to propose a *political* model of foundation."[39] D&G, I submit, echo Detienne's claim when they evoke an Autochthon that is freed by the city by way of a deterritorialization through immanence and without any intervention of transcendence.

According to the vocabulary for the foundation of colonies that develops in the eighth century B.C.E. in connection with the creation of entirely new cities, especially in Sicily and southern Italy, the founder is defined in terms of the activities of clearing the sites in foreign lands for the cities and of settling within traced enclosures. In "Qu'est-ce qu'un site?," Detienne invokes "the care the Founders took to render the site to be colonized desertlike."[40] The foundational act thus amounts to a deterritorialization that detaches the site from all connections to the earth before it is reterritorialized. (The site of colonization, it seems, is a site where *khora* will have made room for topos.) Now, according to Detienne, apart from these two activities a third term defines the founder, with which I return again to my opening reference to what Renan calls the "Greek miracle." This third term is *archegetes.* According to Liddell and Scott's *Greek-English Lexicon,* the *archegetes* is "the first leader, author, especially founder of a city, or family."[41] As a title of Apollo, the term signifies that the god either partook personally in the foundation of colonial cities or showed approval of their creation by humans and that he would stand to protect them. Now, as "the archegetous god: at once the Supreme Leader, Ancestor and Founder" who, from the pan-Hellenic sanctuary of Delphi, that is, the navel (*omphalos*) of the world, dominates the entirety of the foundational activities, Apollo is the model for the human, or psycho-social type, of the founder of colonies. Since Apollo is "the archegetous God" and none other than the "celestial" or "imperial Stranger" (86) invoked by D&G when speaking about the vertical development from on high of the City as a State, a remark about this Greek god par excellence may be warranted.

Nowhere in the whole world could the pregnant Leto find a place to give birth to Apollo and his twin sister, Artemis, because Hera in her jealousy and wrath prohibited the earth to allow the Titaness a place to deliver. Finally, the unhappy Leto found shelter on the small island Ortygia (the island of Quails) in the center of the Cyclades, where she gave birth first to Artemis, who then helped her mother deliver her brother. Born outside Olympus, Apollo is therefore, in a certain sense, an unolympian god. Now, if Hera (who at times is depicted as Mother Earth) could not prevent Leto from delivering her children on this island, it is because she had no jurisdiction over it since the island in question was a floating, or nomadic, rock without any anchorage in the earth, bottomless, as it were. Only after Poseidon anchored it in the absolute center of the four points on the compass did the island, which until then went by the name of Ortygia, or Adelos (the invisible), become Delos (the visible). To return one more time to Blanchot's reference to Vincent van Gogh's saying that he is attached to the Earth, Apollo is thus a god who from the start is also constitutionally detached from the earth. In any event, in gratitude for providing him a place to be born, the god laid the island "down as the center of the Greek world and named it Delos the brilliant."[42] Only after a yearlong sojourn in the land of the Hyperboreans, "on the shores of the ocean, beyond the country of the north Wind," that is, in the extreme north, where the swans that drew his chariot (a present from Zeus) had taken him after his birth, Apollo returned to Greece and made his way to Delphi, where a sanctuary that its people built in honor of the god is called the "navel of the world."[43] Now, it is important to point out that this somewhat unolympian god, who is at the same time the Greek god par excellence, also spent most of his life on earth and among men (paradoxically, it may be precisely his birth on the floating island without attachment to the earth that made it possible for him to dwell on the earth, with a lower case *e*). As the story goes, he was put to two tests: once, he had to "put himself in the position of a slave in the service of mortal masters," and, on another occasion, he had to serve as a shepherd or a cowherd in the service of a king (but also sometimes working for himself).[44] Furthermore, most, though by no means all, of his deeds are on this earth.

With this in mind, let me return to the territorialization and deterritorialization that is involved in the creation of new cities. As Detienne argues, the process of creating cities on cleared land in the Greek world, which the settlers came to inhabit (*oikizein*), is characterized by two levels:

> First in the pantheon yet close to the human world and its cities [the process of territorialization occurs] by way of the activity of divine power, that is, through the God Apollo who shapes the space and from whom originate the gestures and rites by way of which the sites are laid out, marked out, and cut out. For this archegetous god, who has been born in exile on earth, has himself been expelled from the heavens and

> condemned to work among mortals. The career of Apollo, the archegetous god, takes place entirely on the earth of humans, and in the middle of their cities. The gods of Olympus never found any cities in heaven; they are not architects like the Sumerian gods, who trace the plan of the cities which the kings as builders of kingdoms carefully reproduce. The Greek city is never the creation of a god locked on Olympus. Second, the archegetous god in exile is joined by his totally mortal double: the Founder, often an exiled individual himself, who seems to mimic the gestures that Apollo inaugurated.[45]

The founder as "a human type in the Greek world," who is himself also often a stranger and "a mortal homologue of the god of foundation, Apollo Archegetes" exiled from the heavens, the "Celestial Stranger," in short, creates on foreign soil cities that are independent from the motherland and its cities, cities that posit themselves absolutely.[46] They are autochthonous not because they are of the land and the earth but because they have all by themselves and of themselves grounded themselves, deterritorializing the land and reterritorializing it onto a politically grounded community. In "Qu'est-ce qu'un site?," Detienne also points out that the singularity of the political founder is further highlighted by the significant fact that "the dead, the ancestors do not weigh heavily in his luggage."[47]

This is, I conclude, the concept of autochthony that D&G link to the Greek polis, and that answers the question about the sense in which Greece is "the philosopher's territory or philosophy's earth." It is a concept of autochthony distinct from the one encoded by the official obsession with sameness and the fascination with the auto-referential, distinct from, in short, the myth of being born from the earth that dominated the official discourse, especially in Athens. Wrenched from the earth, the philosopher's earth as the deterritorialized par excellence is reterritorialized onto Greece as an earth that is constituted by the free and autochthonous citizens of the polis, an earth that, in practice, has also been much more open to foreigners than the official discourse would seem to allow, which thus also made it possible for a miracle to occur in Greece: the miracle of the birth of philosophy.

4

The Friend, for Example

According to D&G, then, philosophy—this essentially Greek thing—is from its beginning in Greece geophilosophy, that is, a philosophy whose main concern is the earth. As will become clear in a moment, rather than a search for wisdom, philosophy as geophilosophy is not so much "about" the earth, than, from the start, engaged in the earth in a way that entails an unconditional yes to this earth. After having elaborated in the preceding chapters on how "earth" is to be understood here, I now begin looking into the way in which D&G determine the basic features that characterize Greek philosophical thought. According to *What Is Philosophy?*, these are concept creation on a plane of immanence, the conceptual persona of the friend, and the liberation of opinion. Taking my start in a commentary on the "Introduction: The Question Then . . . ," which is devoted primarily to a discussion of the friend, my ultimate aim is to reflect on how these three basic features, or conditions, of philosophy (as a Greek thing both then and now) are linked up with D&G's definition of philosophy as in essence geophilosophy. In other words, how do they devolve from the concept of earth on which we have so far elaborated? As we will see, the earth of philosophy is the ground that requires philosophy to create concepts and to call on the friend and free opinion. As a consequence, rather than a marginal issue in D&G's thought, the earth itself not only stands in the center of their philosophical concerns; it also conditions the three, fundamental traits that characterize philosophy and that make it a Greek thing. In turn, by retracing these traits back to what D&G mean by earth, further light will be shed on how earth is to be understood in both the philosophical and (more narrowly) the sociopolitical senses that D&G distinguish.

As the authors of *What Is Philosophy?* submit, they have always held philosophy to be "the art of forming, inventing, and fabricating concepts" (2). But, at this late hour at which they return to and reflect back on this "old person" (11) that is philosophy itself and on what they have done all their lives, they want to pose the question "what is philosophy?" in a philosophical manner, that is, according to the conditions of philosophy itself. Furthermore, they want to inscribe into the response to this question the occasion, the circumstances, and the landscapes in which it arose, while also taking into account the conceptual personae that are involved in philosophically questioning the nature of philosophy. The conceptual personae are "figurations" of the philosopher within philosophy itself (such as Socrates in the case of Plato) but not the actual "philosopher's [own] representative" (64) as some characters of a philosophical dialogue may be. The conceptual persona is, according to D&G, an intrinsic aspect of philosophy in that it "intervenes between chaos and the diagrammatic features of the plane of immanence and also between the plane and the intensive features of the concepts that happen to populate it" (75). Since what they want is, indeed, to ask and to respond to the question of what philosophy is " 'between friends,' . . . or as a challenge when confronting the enemy" (2), the philosopher as friend is the persona to which, in the "Introduction," most of their attention is devoted. How "informing, inventing, fabricating concepts" is to be understood and, especially, what D&G mean by concepts will only be clarified a bit later, along with the notion of the "conceptual personae" itself, which are needed by concepts and "play a part in their definition" (2). For the time being, I only retain D&G's claim that, in particular, "*Friend* is one such persona [and that it is] even said to reveal the Greek origin of philo-sophy: other civilizations had sages, but the Greeks introduce these 'friends' who are not just more modest sages" (2–3).

By invoking the friend as a persona who must be present in asking what philosophy is, D&G not only pretend to philosophize in a Greek way; they also determine philosophy itself as something essentially Greek, something that is significantly distinct from what obtains in other instituted cultures, that is, civilizations. Without yet clarifying how they wish to understand certain terms, the point they are about to make is unmistakable: the Greek philosopher as a friend and philosophy as something that takes place amongst friends are radically different from the sage and the sage's teaching to his pupils. D&G write: "The Greeks are said to have ratified the death of the sage and to have replaced him with philosophers—the friends of wisdom, those who seek wisdom but do not formally possess it" (3; trans. mod.). However, the wisdom for which the philosophers strive is no longer that of the oriental sage: "Wisdom has changed a great deal," as D&G observe (ibid.). Indeed, it may have changed to such a degree that even the term *sophia* in *philosophia* is no longer fully appropriate to designate it. Recall that, according to Plato in *Cratylus,* even the word "*sophia* (wisdom) is very dark, and appears not to be of native growth [*xenikoteron*]."[1] In any event, as D&G aver in a reference to Nietzsche, philosophy at its origin in the pre-Socratics "borrow[ed] the sage's mask," "carry[ing] out a vast diversion of wisdom" by undermining the sages' reference to a transcendent order and placing wisdom "at the service of pure immanence" (43–44).

Now, in making the distinction between the philosopher and the sage, D&G rely explicitly on Alexandre Kojève, even though their references to Marcel Detienne's *The Masters of Truth in Archaic Greece* and to Jean-Pierre Vernant's *The Origin of Greek Thought* in their evocation of the first philosophers make evident that Kojève is not their sole source on this subject matter. Citing Vernant, they write that the first philosophers "who institute[d] a plane of immanence like a sieve stretched over the chaos . . . contrast with sages, who are religious personae, priests, because they conceive of the institution of an always transcendent order imposed from outside by a great despot or by one god higher than the others, inspired by Eris, pursuing wars that go beyond any agon and hatreds that object in advance to the trials of rivalry" (43).[2] A similar point is made in *The Masters of Truth in Archaic Greece,* where Detienne outlines the history of the evolution of the figure of the master of truth, from the inspired poet and the seer of mythical times and religious thought to the philosopher (first and foremost, Parmenides), but also the contemporaneous wise men of the philosophico-religious sects. Because of the direct vision that the goddess grants him of *Aletheia,* the philosopher, in some respect, still resembles the magus, but, whereas the latter "had lived apart from the polis, on the periphery of society, . . . the philosopher, by contrast, was subject to the urban regime and therefore to the demands of publicity. He was obliged to leave the sanctuary of revelation."[3] Not only is his truth thus "open to challenge if not to verification," but the first philosophers also have to take *doxa* into account in distinction, in particular, from the sages of the philosophico-religious sects for whom interactions with the world of the plurality of *doxai* is to be shunned.[4] In contrast to the magus, or sage, who was an individual and whose efforts consisted in acquiring individual wisdom, the first philosophers are public figures, steeped in the milieu of immanence of the polis. But let me return to the explicitly acknowledged source of D&G's discussion of the difference between the sage and the philosopher, namely, Kojève. In *Tyranny and Wisdom,* Kojève broaches, indeed, the distinction between the philosopher and the sage but, paradoxically, limits himself—admittedly "for want of wise men" (172)—to merely characterizing the figure of the philosopher.[5] For Kojève, the philosopher by definition does not possess wisdom, and, therefore, he is, by definition again, supposed to devote all his life to the search for wisdom, as opposed to the sage who is already in full possession of it.[6] Indeed, as Kojève writes, "philosophy is by definition something other than Wisdom: it necessarily involves 'subjective certainties' which are not *the* Truth; or in other words are 'prejudices'."[7] But D&G point to still another difference between the sage and the philosopher: they hold that "the old oriental sage thinks, perhaps, in

Figures, whereas the philosopher invents and thinks the Concept" (3). This distinction, modalized by a "perhaps," has at first a very traditional ring, since it seems to echo the familiar oppositions of intuition versus analytical or conceptual thinking, image versus concept, and so forth. However, since for D&G concepts are not discursive entities, and figures not simply images, this distinction may also have connotations that distinguish it from the way it is commonly understood.[8]

For the time being, D&G do not pursue the question of this difference but center on the notion of the friend, since it is especially "difficult to know what *friend* signifies, even and especially among the Greeks" (3). "The question is important," they note, "because the friend who appears in philosophy no longer stands for an extrinsic persona, an example or empirical circumstance, but rather for a presence that is intrinsic to thought, a condition of possibility of thought itself, a living category, a transcendental lived experience" (3; trans. mod.). The friend for the Greeks, that is, insofar as it is one of the main traits of philosophy, is a conceptual persona intrinsic to thought itself. D&G refer to the friend as a "transcendental determination" (4), in other words, as an a priori condition for there to be philosophy. In passing I note that the ease with which they speak of transcendental experience and determinations is somewhat surprising given that in Kant and Husserl the transcendental is immanent *to* consciousness, or subjectivity, and hence, as they argue in "Example 3," the modern way of reintroducing the transcendent (45). Although they do not say so explicitly, the two other features of philosophy as a Greek thing—the creation of concepts on a plane of immanence and the liberation of opinion—have a similar status: they are also a priori transcendental conditions without which there is no such a thing as philosophical thought. Furthermore, if the friend is a conceptual persona intrinsic to thought itself, this also means that "it is thought itself that requires the thinker to be a friend so that thought is divided up within itself and can be exercised" (69). If thought is to be divided within itself, rather than smoothly relating to itself encapsulated apart from any exchange with the exterior, and thus something that at all moments must be performed ("exercised"), or enacted, the friend as an Other with whom to vie must be intrinsic to philosophy itself. Before I pursue this thread, let me only point out that the friend is a figure, as it were, who has a "competent intimacy" or "material taste" (3) for wisdom, truth, and the concept in a manner not unlike that which the carpenter or cabinetmaker has for wood. The friend in philosophy is a persona who is very competent in concepts, who has the know-how (*le philosophe s'y connait*) for concepts—he is "expert in concepts" (ibid.), as Hugh Tomlinson and Graham Burchell translate—but a sense of expertise that is based on a taste for concepts, on a sensible disposition rather than intellectual skills. Allow me to anticipate that, with this interpretation of the friend in philosophy as something Greek, a very specific way of looking at philosophy comes into view that we will see confirmed later, when concepts are defined as nondiscursive and philosophy is radically set off from the sciences. Indeed, philosophy, this Greek something that consists above all in the creation of concepts, is nonetheless nothing primarily rationalistic or cerebral.

If the friend as the conceptual persona of the philosopher in philosophy itself is "the friend or lover of wisdom . . . striving for it potentially rather than actually possessing it" (4), this friend is in philosophy the analog of the Athenian citizen, a free man, an equal among equals. Indeed, D&G speak of the societies of friends that emerge in Greece as societies of equals (ibid.). Recall Cleisthenes's reform, which led to the formation in Greece of broad, civilian solidarity. As Meier notes, "this solidarity furnished the basis for the various attempts to secure participation in civic affairs and was itself reinforced by such participation. It is not clear, however, whether it was understood as friendship." Historically speaking, "the idea that the members of the different classes should be united by friendship," Meier says, "acquired topical importance only when the city was faced with the threat of civil war arising from the struggle for control of the political order."[9] As Meier has shown in an analysis of Aeschylus's *Euminedes,* the idea of friendship between the citizens of the polis, which arose at that moment and made friendship a requirement for being a citizen, rather than just "a matter of interpersonal relations," came with the demand that the citizen no longer direct enmity "inward, but outward, in a spirit of solidarity."[10] Based on "a new, polis-oriented distinction between friend and foe," civic friendship thus became in Greece an intrinsic aspect of the new civic solidarity—as it is expressed by the formula *koinophiles dianoia,* that is, "love directed to the whole (the *koinon*) and mutual friendship within the community"—that arose in times of looming civil war.[11] Now, it is also the case that this ideal of friendship among citizens as equals did not exclude serious strife.[12] I return, therefore, to D&G's contention that the conceptual persona of the friend in philosophy as a lover of wisdom also makes him as such a claimant (*un prétendant*), that is, one who makes a claim to the same thing all others assert, as well. Yet, as a claimant, if "that of which he claims to be the friend [is] the Thing to which he lays claim," namely wisdom in the case of the philosopher, rather than "the third party [*le tiers*]," then any other, inevitably, "becomes a rival" in an agonal strife. D&G continue: "Friendship would then involve competitive distrust of the rival as much as amorous striving toward the object of desire. The basic point about friendship is that the two friends are like claimant and rival (but who could tell them apart?)" (4).[13] Undoubtedly, Nietzsche's essay "Homer's Contest" is on D&G's mind here. In this essay, Nietzsche argued that *agon*—contest, or competitive strife—is the basic trait of the Greek world as a world that sought to promote the equality of its citizens even at the price of ostracism (which, by the way, is believed to have been instituted by Cleisthenes), in other words, of exiling anyone who excelled in deeds or word so much that no one was equal to him anymore.[14] In short, if to say friend is to say equal, then the fact that the friend vies for the same thing—truth, wisdom, and so on—inevitably makes him into a rival, or even an enemy in the strong sense, a *polemios*.[15]

Thus understood, the friend is not only the conceptual persona par excellence of philosophy—indeed, as the reference in this context to Blanchot's reflections on friendship seems to suggest, all other conceptual persona in philosophy are only variations, modifications, or opposites of the figure of the friend—but also, inasmuch as the friend is, as an equal, also a rival in the strife for wisdom, he or she is also the first distinctive trait that seems to make philosophy a specifically Greek thing. Indeed, friendship is the condition for philosophy to be a public thing, something that is realized in practical fashion in making philosophy together—*symphilosophein*—in an agonal strife, rather than something personal or private like wisdom. D&G write: "It is in this first aspect that philosophy seems to be something Greek and coincides with the contribution of cities: the formation of societies of friends or equals but also the promotion of relationships of rivalry between and within them, the contest between claimants in every sphere . . . even in thought, which finds its condition not only in the friend but in the claimant and the rival (the dialectic Plato defined as *amphisbetesis*)" (4).[16] The "transcendental determinations" of the friend, lover, claimant, and rival brought to light by the search for an answer to the "question internal to the conditions of thought as such" (4)—that is, the question "what is philosophy?"—shows this first characteristic to be something essentially Greek since philosophy (with the conceptual persona of the philosopher as a friend) presupposes a society of thinkers who, as friends of wisdom in distinction from sages, are engaged in an agonal strife for truth or wisdom that at the same time makes them rivals.[17]

A footnote in the chapter on "Geophilosophy" about Georg Simmel's notion of "pure sociability, 'before and beyond any particular content,'" requires our attention at this point (223n4). The source is an essay entitled "Die Geselligkeit (Beispiel der Reinen oder Formalen Soziologie)," in which Simmel makes the distinction between socialization (*Vergesellschaftung*) and sociability (*Geselligkeit*). Whereas socialization concerns the content of the interactions of human beings in society who, under the pressures of the necessities of life and the exigencies of praxis, "enter into co-existence with one another, that is, into an action that at the same time is an action for, with, and against one another," sociability is a phenomenon of society that arises through "a kind of intellectual function of absolutely considerable importance," which abstracts the pure form of human interaction from the forces and interests that are at the service of life and endows it with an independence from all these exigencies and practical matters.[18] Detached from "the flux of mere life and the matter of the latter that gives it its seriousness," the forms of life created by the realities of life gain a life of their own and become a value in themselves in the shape of sociability as "the proper 'society' " of human beings interacting for, with, or against one another.[19] In full abstraction from the seriousness of life, "being with, for, or against others" acquires a formal life of its own, "freed of all rootedness in a [particular] content."[20] As opposed to the ordinary forms of socialization, sociability creates "a sociologically ideal world," an "artificial world," "a social work of art," as it were, in which the relation between human beings is freed from the common ends of existence and the energies that were directed toward the pursuit of those constraints can now be acted out in ludic fashion. Sociability thus represents "an ideal sociological world."[21] Sociability, Simmel holds, is "essentially democratic"; however artificial, "the world of sociability is the only one in which a democracy of people who enjoy equal rights is possible without frictions."[22]

Is what Simmel calls sociability not precisely that which characterizes D&G's societies of friends and equals, which, as we have seen, is one of the socio-political conditions for the emergence of philosophy in Greece, and as a result of which the friend becomes a conceptual persona intrinsic to philosophy itself? Keeping in mind Simmel's insistence on the freedom of these real societies from the constraints of existence, are these societies not also, I ask, the space in which its participants are set free as autochthons in D&G's understanding of this term? Furthermore, can one not also see here that it is precisely philosophy's understanding of "earth" as a sociopolitical space created by its free and equal members' interactions that requires the friend to be an essential feature of philosophical thought as an essentially Greek thing?

5

Taking Flight

I now proceed to the second trait of philosophy, that is, the creation of concepts, that also makes it, according to D&G, something essentially Greek. From the start let me emphasize that it is not *creation* that distinguishes philosophy from the other forms of thought that are the sciences and the arts but only the creation of *concepts*. At the very end of the book, when D&G point out that philosophy's creation of concepts responds to the task of philosophy to "teach us to conceive," as opposed to the sciences that "teach us to know" and the arts that teach us "to feel" (218), it is obvious that concepts are intrinsically linked to this one form of thought. Philosophy, which is as creative as any of the other forms of thought, is one such form whose distinguishing trait is the creation of concepts. As is manifest from a long quotation from Nietzsche's *The Will to Power* that states that the philosopher's first task is to "*make* and *create* [concepts], present them and make them convincing [*hinstellen und zu ihnen überreden*]," D&G take this distinctive feature of the form of thought that is philosophy, at first, from Nietzsche (5).[1] Now, in conformity with the classical valorization of *auto-poiesis* over *techne,* such making or creating is not judged to be simply a forming, inventing, or fabricating of concepts, because concepts are not necessarily forms, discoveries, or products. Indeed, following Raymond Ruyer (whose work *Néo-Finalisme* has been, as D&G explicitly acknowledge, a decisive source for their understanding of what a concept is), creation, or what Ruyer terms "invention" or "action," is never of the order of "a function [*fonctionnement*], that is, of a whole of movements according to the ready-made linkages of a machine, or the differences of the potentiality of a field of forces."[2] Creation never takes place in the shape of a running or working order of an operation, procedure, or mechanism. More precisely, rather than giving rise to "a pure succession of causes and effects that can be numbered, and that follow upon one another in a well-defined spatiotemporal order without any possibility of reversibility, and that are, by definition, unable to survey [*se survoler*] themselves," invention is a "meaningful activity, free, and creative of value," that is, "the creation of form, and not of a functioning."[3] Concepts are certainly not the product of an operation of abstraction or generalization (11). Although D&G hold in the "Introduction" that philosophy, in a rigorous sense, is "the discipline that involves *creating* concepts" and that "the object of philosophy is to create concepts that are always new" (5), this second distinguishing trait of philosophy will, at first, only be provisionally explored and, moreover, only within the limits of the context of the question of the friend. So, before I engage in a more technical discussion of the creation of concepts based on Chapter 1, "What Is a Concept?," I first pursue the issue as it is presented in the introductory pages of the work, in which the emphasis lies on the creation of concepts as it pertains to the friend. Using the Aristotelian expression of "potentiality," D&G write that "the philosopher is the concept's friend; he is potentiality of the concept [*il est en puissance de concept*]" (5). In a first approximation, it must be noted that D&G's claim that philosophy consists in the creation of concepts has a rather familiar ring. Indeed, numerous thinkers have equated the specificity of Greek philosophical thought, and Western philosophical thought in general, with the formation and the work of the concept. In advance of a more detailed discussion of the notion, it is necessary therefore to evoke in a manner as condensed and as broad as possible what a concept is, and, so, I must turn at least briefly to the definition our authors provide of the concept in the first chapter of the book. As we will see, what they understand by concept is not the concept as we know it. And, if this is so, what they understand by *creation* (of concepts) and by *philosophy* as the discipline of creating concepts will also have a different meaning from the one these terms ordinarily have. But, first, what is a concept in the common philosophical sense? Although the notion of concept (*rhema*) is already introduced by Plato in the context of his theory of ideas, it is not an idea itself insofar as the latter remains transcendent. On the contrary, a concept is commonly held to be part of the human intellect. It is a means of knowing what is (and hence referential), and, as such, it is an intellectual object with an identical content, produced by thought insofar as it detaches a set of individual things from their immediate reality, thus making it possible to grasp them as what they are in themselves, that is, the unity that determines their manifold. A concept names what is universal about a thing, or things, and immobilizes them, as it were, in their unitary essence, or ideality. To illustrate this I take my example from Kant, for whom concepts are explicitly linked to the cognition of objects. Without concepts, however imperfect or obscure they may be, there is no such thing as cognition. Concepts play this crucial mediating function in cognition, because a concept, Kant writes, "is this *one* consciousness that unifies the manifold that has been successively intuited, and then also reproduced, into one representation."[4] The concept has this significant role on the basis of its form. It "is always something general, and something that serves as a rule . . . for our cognition of outer [and inner] appearances by means of the unity of the manifold that is thought through it."[5]

Before I make a first attempt to define "concept" in D&G's sense, a brief note about a surprising connection between Idea and concept that they make in the "Introduction" to *What Is Philosophy?* may be warranted. They submit: "If philosophy is this continuous creation of concepts, then obviously the question arises not only of what a concept is as philosophical Idea but also of the nature of the other creative Ideas that are not concepts and that are due to the arts and sciences, which have their own history and becoming and which have their own variable relationships with one another and with philosophy" (8). The concept is thus characterized as a "philosophical Idea." Yet the concept itself is not the same as an Idea but only a form of it—that is, a philosophical Idea—for, indeed, it also follows from this passage that what the sciences create, namely functives, are scientific Ideas and that the percepts and affects of the arts are aesthetic Ideas. "Idea" thus only serves as a comprehensive term for all three creations.[6] But what about this overarching role of "Idea"? Written with a capital "I," it is more than unlikely that D&G make here only a cursory use of the term "Idea." I leave this issue in abeyance for the moment.

As D&G themselves admit in *What Is Philosophy?*, it is difficult to determine what a concept is as they understand it because of the "long series of misunderstandings about the concept. It is true that the concept is fuzzy or vague not because it lacks an outline but because it is vagabond, nondiscursive, moving about on a plane of immanence" (143). Taking my departure in the first chapter of the book, "What Is a Concept?," the first definition of a concept for D&G is a highly abstract one. If it is abstract, it is, primarily, because the features that characterize it are not a function of the manifold of an object that the concept would serve to render intelligible. Indeed, the emphasis in the definition that they propose in the chapter in question lies on the concept itself. But it is an abstract definition for still another reason. What D&G state about the nature of the concept remains abstract as long as its other side, a side that is distinct from the concept but at the same time inseparable from it, namely, the surface or plane that cuts through multiplicity and on which concepts are created, has not been evoked. Once this other side of the concept has been brought into play, I may have to rework this first definition of the concept. For now, however, I follow their definition of the concept as a whole made up of a finite multiplicity of heterogeneous components that it totalizes while remaining fragmentary, because these components are the result of a selective cut performed in what is to be totalized. "Defined by the sum of its components" (15–16) that are articulated within it, that is, linked and joined together within its contours, the concept is a whole with irregular borders. What characterizes a concept primarily is thus the *consistency* with which its heterogeneous components are tied to one another and rendered inseparable. This consistency and inseparableness of the distinct components within the concept are not logical. The relations between its components are not relationships of comprehension, or extension, but are ordered according to their spatial interrelations, topologically, that is. Each component "partially overlaps, has a zone of neighborhood [*zone de voisinage*], or a threshold of indiscernibility, with another one" (19). Thresholds, zones, and bridges not only are the joints between concepts but also determine the concept's internal consistency. In short, although the internal consistency of the concept is intelligible, it is not rational; it is based on the network of the passages that have been cut between the partially overlapping components. For what they understand by concept in distinction from what this term commonly means in philosophy, the following illuminating example is certainly helpful: "The concept of a bird is found not in its genus or species but in the composition of its postures, colors, and songs: something indiscernible that is not so much synesthetic as syneidetic" (20). Now, if a concept thus understood "is a heterogenesis" (ibid.), that is, an ordering of a multiplicity of dissimilar components and characterized by the consistency that it brings about between them, a concept is also a happening; more precisely, it has event-character. The creation of concepts is the creation of events of thought. Qua events, what D&G name concept does not have the logical reality of a concept according to Aristotle, or of what Kant calls a form of the understanding. Nor is the concept, as already said, of the order of a general or abstract idea. As D&G note, for Plato to have developed his theory of the Ideas, he first had to have the concept of the Idea. The reality of the concept as the reality of philosophy itself is of a different nature than traditionally held. As events, concepts have an ontological status of their own, first of all, the status of singularities.

Now, when D&G write that "the concept is an incorporeal, even though it is incarnated or effectuated in bodies," adding that the concept is an "act of thought" that "speaks the event, not the essence or the thing—pure Event, a hecceity, an entity" (21), it becomes clear that their notion of concept is indebted at least to some extent to a grand philosophical school in antiquity that, for having separated itself (at least as far as physics is concerned) from the common tradition shared by all the schools that emerged in the aftermath of Socratic teaching, was considered an inadmissible scandal that drew the unanimous condemnation of the entirety of the trade. I am speaking of ancient Stoicism accused by its adversaries of materialism even though as Eric Weil has noted there does not exist in any of the texts anything that allows one to speak of materialism. In fact, as Weil argues, their theory consists in arguing that anything that acts, and anything that is subjected to action, including truth, the Good, and *pneuma,* or God, has a corporeal nature.[7] But the Stoics also acknowledge the existence of incorporeals, of which the four most important are space, time, the void, and that of which one speaks, or the expressible (*lekton*). D&G's understanding of the concept is indebted above all to this latter part of this old doctrine which, according to Emile Bréhier, who is their source in this matter, existed in purity before it became subsequently diluted by the peripatetic and Platonic elements in the later forms of Stoicism.[8] Asked by Claire Parnet why write about the Stoics, Deleuze responds in *Dialogues II* that:

> The Stoics' strength lay in making a line of separation pass—no longer between the sensible and the intelligible, or between the soul and the body, but where no one had seen it before—between physical depth and metaphysical surface. Between things and events. Between states of things and compounds, causes, souls and bodies, actions and passions, qualities and substances on the one hand, and, on the other, events or impassive, unqualifiable, incorporeal Effects, infinitives which result from these amalgams, which are attributed to these states of things, which are expressed in propositions.[9]

Already in the *Logic of Sense,* Deleuze had quoted Bréhier's work on this Stoic doctrine, according to which there are two radically distinct planes of being: "on the one hand, profound and real being, namely force, and on the other hand, the plane of facts that play at the surface of being, and which constitute an unlimited multiplicity of incorporeal beings that are without links."[10] Although these incorporeal or unreal beings are fully separate from real beings and their proprieties in that they are only attributed to them (they are *katagoremata*) as things that happen to them—for instance (the example is from Sextus Empiricus), "when the scalpel cuts the flesh, the first body does not produce a new propriety in the second body, but [only] the new attribute of having been cut"[11]—they are events, occurrences, happenings. In *Dialogues II,* Deleuze speaks of them as "a sort of incorporeal vapour" that arises from real beings and their bodily struggle, which "no longer consists in qualities, in actions or in passions, in causes acting upon one another, but in results of these actions and passions, in effects which result from all these causes together."[12] This incorporeal vapour of the "pure, impassive, incorporeal events, on the surface of things," that rises from the state of real and corporeal things and that "skims over it [*le survole*]," that flies over it, is also the element of the concepts, which, as we will see, are not only events on surfaces, or planes, but also themselves domains that are intrinsically constituted by an "operation" of skimming over, survey, or *survol*.[13]

As an incorporeal, the concepts created by philosophy thus hover in the vapor of the events that, according to the Stoics, arise from the surface of corporeal things. They are like a superstructural stratum on top of the infrastructural of the real. This stratum is, as the issue of the incorporeals suggests, one of pure meaning. D&G assert, indeed, that the concept "is the event as pure sense that immediately runs through the components" that are gathered within it in consistent fashion (144). Now, as D&G hold, in philosophy concepts are created only in view of problems "without which they would have no meaning" (16)—"the concept is indeed a solution" (80); the creation of concepts is the creation of singular events on the level of cognition. If concepts have no meaning except with respect to problems, then the implication is that concept creation, as Deleuze holds in *Negotiations,* must be necessary rather than arbitrary and, furthermore, that by responding to "real problems" they must also have a certain strangeness about them.[14] What such problems are, and in particular whence they arise, will have to be clarified later. First, however, let us take note of the definition of philosophy that D&G, after having explained that philosophy is the discipline for creating concepts, offer a couple of pages later in the "Introduction," a definition they call "decisive": philosophy, they submit, is "knowledge [*connaissance*] through pure concepts" (7). Does this mean that their understanding of concept is not different from the classical concept in question after all? And, if not, in what sense does one have to understand "knowledge," if it cannot be knowledge of objects? Indeed, as we have already seen from the definition that D&G provide of the concept, the latter is defined by its internal consistency: "The concept speaks the event, not the essence or the thing" (21). It is "pure Event, a hecceity, an entity" (ibid.). A first consequence of understanding the concept in this manner as "an act of thought" (ibid.) is that the concept "has no *reference*" (22). Rather "it is self-referential; it posits itself and its object at the same time as it is created" (ibid.). I will come back to this aspect of the concept a bit later when I address the constitutive nature of the concept as survey, and self-survey, and D&G's emphasis on the concept's autonomy. A second consequence is that "the concept is not discursive, and philosophy is not a discursive formation, because it does not link propositions together" (ibid.). The concept is not a proposition since "propositions are defined by their reference, which concerns not the Event but rather a relationship with a state of affairs or body and with the conditions of this relationship" (ibid.). Propositions and reference are, D&G argue, the turf of the sciences. So, a concept in D&G's understanding is definitely not referential. It does not give us to know an object. If they can nonetheless speak of "knowledge through pure concepts," knowledge must consist of something other than knowledge of objects. It can, therefore, only concern the relation of the concept to itself.

I recall that the definition of the concept provided so far remained abstract because the plane on which the concepts are created and operate has not yet been thematized. Indeed, after having held philosophy to be "knowledge through pure concepts," D&G write:

> There is no reason to oppose knowledge through concepts and the construction of concepts within possible experience on the one hand and through intuition on the other. For, according to the Nietzschean verdict, you will know nothing through concepts unless you have first created them—that is, constructed them in an intuition specific to them: a field, a plane, and a ground that must not be confused with them but that shelters their seeds and the personae who cultivate them. (7)

In short then, the knowledge that pure philosophical concepts provide is not one of objects or of states of affairs (this is the resort of the sciences). Given the fact that they conceive of concepts as self-referential, as "knowing themselves," as it were, the knowledge that they provide is a knowledge that is immanent to themselves and to the plane on which they are created. From the passage one can also draw the conclusion that the knowledge in question, rather than discursive and propositional, is of the order of some sort of intuition, at least in a Nietzschean sense.

Before I return to the "Introduction" and the question of the creation of concepts to refine in greater detail how "creation" and "concept" are to be taken here, I wish already to take stock briefly of what D&G's conception of the concept means for philosophy. I wish to address, however briefly, the enormous stakes of this reconception of the philosophical concept. Traditionally, a concept is understood as a representation, or notion, that is formed in the mind by external objects or experiences to which it thus relates, which serves the understanding or cognitive mastery of the objects. However, according to D&G, understanding objects is not the objective of the concepts created by philosophy. For D&G, a concept that serves to make objects cognitively intelligible is the traditional, philosophical concept of the concept. Indeed, what they suggest is that this understanding of concept as being at the service of the knowledge of things is the scientific or metaphysical conception of the concept and not philosophical at all. By arguing that the concept is not logical and, hence, that it has no reference to objects—that, furthermore, it is not propositional and discursive—D&G separate metaphysics, understood since Aristotle as the knowledge of cause and definition, from philosophy. Metaphysics thus expulsed from philosophy becomes the domain proper of the sciences whose "functives" and "prospects" (as opposed to "concepts") are, indeed, referential, and whose operational mode is discursive. Indeed, as is made clear on the last pages of *What Is Philosophy?,* science alone operates in a way "which constitute[s] an activity of knowing and refer[s] to a faculty of knowledge as the third layer of a brain-subject that is no less creative than the other two [that is, philosophy and the arts]. Knowledge is neither a form nor a force but a *function*" (214–15).[15] Only the sciences operate on "a plane of knowledge (reference)" (215). Now, traditionally at least, science and the discourse of knowledge have, at least to a large extent, been confounded with philosophy. It thus becomes clear that with their new understanding of the philosophical concept D&G are undertaking nothing less than a massive reorganization or reshuffling of the disciplines and their different commands. Metaphysics is science, or the ground of science, and is separated off from philosophy; the whole problematic of beauty is extracted from philosophy, as well, and is made into the specific resort of the arts. But if this is the case, the question that D&G have set out to answer, that is, "what is philosophy?," becomes all the more pressing. If, indeed, D&G's agenda consists in determining the three forms of thought whose "three planes, along with their elements, are irreducible" (216)—namely, philosophy, the sciences, and the arts in all their intrinsic purity—which philosophy has neglected to do from early on, with the result that the specific task of what philosophy is supposed to accomplish has been lost sight of, the question of what philosophy is becomes a task in itself. What is it specifically that the Greeks brought into the world, who, notwithstanding the fact that from early on they also intermixed philosophy with metaphysics and the sciences, had, according to D&G, "it seems . . . a clear-enough idea of science, which was not confused with philosophy: it was a knowledge of the cause, of the definition, a sort of function already" (147)?[16] What, then, is philosophy if, as the creation of concepts, it is in an absolute sense radically distinct from metaphysics, in other words, from science, and from the doctrine of beauty, that is, from the arts? D&G write that "the concept belongs to philosophy and only to philosophy" (34). With this we are back again at the question of what it means for philosophy to be the discipline of creating concepts.

Another aspect of the concept that I only briefly mentioned when I spoke of it as an incorporeal is that it brings about the consistency and inseparability of the finite number of components that it totalizes by traversing them "*by a point of absolute survey at infinite speed.* . . . The 'survey' [*survol*] is the state of the concept or its specific infinity, although the infinities may be larger or smaller according to the number of components, thresholds and bridges. In this sense the concept is act of thought, it is thought operating at infinite (although greater or lesser) speed" (21). Indeed, "each concept [is to] be considered as the point of coincidence, condensation or accumulation of its own components" (20). The "conceptual point" accomplishes this by "constantly" or "endlessly traversing [*parcourir*]" its components in a movement that knows no rest so as to achieve an immediate co-presence of all its components or variations in "an order without distance" (20–21).

Skimming over, surveyance, or overflight are an intrinsic feature of the concept and translate the French word "*survol,*" a notion that D&G do not presume to have originated. Rather, they explicitly acknowledge that they have borrowed this feature of the concept from Ruyer's work on neo-finalism. Before further discussing their conception of the concept, therefore, let me first recapitulate as succinctly as possible how Ruyer understands "*survol,*" or for that matter "*enveloppement,*" another term that D&G sometimes use. In *Néo-Finalisme,* the notion of survey is introduced as a function of Ruyer's attempt to account for "primary consciousness," or "organic consciousness," which is distinct from, and ontologically prior to, consciousness in a Cartesian sense, that is, consciousness directed upon objects, including itself as an object, that as a "second consciousness" derives from "primary consciousness."[17] Concerning multiplicities, the prime role of the survey constitutive of primal consciousness is to organize their elements into unities, that is, wholes that are signifying and meaningful by way of an activity that Ruyer characterizes as finalist. All finalist activity, he argues, implies a unity that skims over a subordinated multiplicity by which it becomes realized in the first place. In any event, primary consciousness represents "an absolute form, or an absolute domain that skims over itself" and that constructs itself by surveying itself.[18] For Ruyer, survey is characteristic not only of consciousness but also more fundamentally of life itself as constituted by what he calls, borrowing the term from Samuel Alexander, "pure *self-enjoyment.*"[19]

But in order not only to realize the extent to which Ruyer's notion of survey is instrumental to understanding what D&G advance about the nature of the concept and the plane of immanence on which it accomplishes consistency, but also to glimpse how Ruyer's vitalist and finalist thought may continue to inform their answer to the question "what is philosophy?," a more detailed exposition of what "survey" accomplishes is certainly in order. As a finalist activity with respect to multiplicities, survey creates the latter's unity as an absolute unity and does so in an immediate fashion. Rather than being linked to itself by way of a process of progressive, cognitive approximation, the "absolute survey as the primary type of all linkage" achieves the common existence of all the elements of a multiplicity in the shape of an "immediate form," which Ruyer also qualifies as "true form" and an "absolute domain" that accomplishes the synthesis of multiplicity from within, that is, without needing any external position from which a comprehending light could be shed on it.[20] The survey is, as Ruyer holds, "not dimensional."[21] Hence, Ruyer's further suggestion that the synthesis that creates true form is "an absolute surface, a tableau that reads itself," both "structure and idea, eidos in the double sense of the word."[22] The whole that a survey thus totalizes is "directly conscious of itself"; it "possesses itself [*auto-possession*]."[23] It is in this sense that such a whole can be said to be an absolute or true form. The survey that accomplishes such a form by immediately linking all the elements of a multiplicity into an organic whole is thus another name for immediate consciousness, a consciousness and a knowledge that are not reflective and that involve no outside point from which the totalization would be accomplished. As will become clear hereafter, all the defining traits of "survey" as they have been established by Ruyer are at work in D&G's theory about the philosophical concept. What they call concept has all the looks of what Ruyer terms absolute or true form.[24]

In distinction from the propositions in the sciences, which proceed by way of a succession within spatiotemporal coordinates with the effect of coordinating them with referents, the concept, according to D&G, totalizes its components by skimming through them at more or less infinite speed. "The problem of [philosophical] thought is infinite speed," D&G tell us (36). The concept totalizes its components at one stroke, as it were! If philosophy is knowledge through pure concepts, this knowledge takes place by way of the very act of the concept that totalizes its components without mediation, in one go, that is, also at infinite speed. Since D&G also evoke the infinite speed with which conceptual personae pass through the components of a concept "in a single instant" (132), the notion of infinite speed highlights the instantaneity peculiar to immediacy, thus replacing this more classical term. In the chapter "Functives and Concepts," it is shown that the sciences, by contrast, relinquish the infinite speed of the concept and operate a "fantastic *slowing down*," a stoppage, a "freeze-frame," through which they secure referentiality. A functive, which in the sciences replaces the concept, is "a Slow-motion [*une Ralentie*]"(118) by way of which the sciences become able to penetrate matter with propositions. Compared to the sciences, philosophy, according to *A Thousand Plateaus,* is at best, indeed, a "minor science."[25] But what does all this tell us about philosophy and the concept? Roughly speaking, philosophy as the creation of concepts is thought conceived exclusively as the pure Event of the ordering of chaos in view of the problems that such ordering solves. More precisely, philosophy is again and again the always singular event of structuring chaos by erecting a plane that cuts through it and that philosophy populates with its concepts. So, concept creation takes place, as already mentioned, on a plane of immanence. I will return to this question a bit later, but at this point I wish to point out already that it is in exploring what is meant by the plane of immanence that we will be able to see how D&G's conception of the earth of philosophy requires concept creation to be the second defining trait of philosophy as a Greek thing.

With this I circle back once again to the "Introduction," first, however, only to pursue further the question of what philosophy is if essentially it is the creation of concepts. If this is what philosophy is, then "we can at least see what philosophy is not: it is not contemplation, reflection, or communication. This is the case even though it may sometimes believe it is one or other of these, as a result of the capacity of every discipline to produce its own illusions and to hide behind its own peculiar smokescreen" (6). All three of these "actions or passions" (ibid.)—contemplation, reflection, communication—are what Kant calls "transcendental illusions," as it were, that philosophy itself inevitably engenders. Indeed, rather than constituting philosophy as a discipline, these three "actions or passions" are only, according to D&G, "machines for constituting Universals in every discipline. The Universals of contemplation, and then of reflection, are like two illusions through which philosophy has already passed in its dream of dominating the other disciplines [that is, in the capacity of *regina scientarum*]" (6–7). This dream is the transcendental illusion of "objective idealism and subjective idealism" (7). A bit later in the text, when D&G return to the question of the "objectality of contemplation, subject of reflection, and intersubjectivity of communication" as "the three figures of philosophy" (92), the term "figure" unmistakably suggests that such understanding of philosophy is a misconception to be attributed to the sciences and religion. Let me linger for a brief moment on the assumption that philosophy is communication. This assumption, indeed, concerns the notion of opinion (*doxa*) to which we will have to return later since it is related to the third characteristic that makes philosophy a Greek thing. Jürgen Habermas, undoubtedly, is the main target of D&G's remarks on communication.

Philosophy, they hold, does not "find any final refuge in communication, which only works under the sway of opinions in order to create 'consensus' and not concepts" (6).[26] Philosophy understood as communication, that is, as "the idea of a Western democratic conversation between friends," is an idea that "comes, perhaps, from the Greeks, but they distrusted it so much, and subjected it to such harsh treatment, that the concept was more like the ironical soliloquy bird that surveyed [*survolait*] the battlefield of destroyed rival opinions (the drunken guests at the banquet)" (ibid.). As we have seen, friends as rivals are also enemies, and the contest, rather than being about accomplishing a consensus, is about the creation of always new concepts. In *Negotiations,* Deleuze remarks that "consensus is an ideal that guides opinion and has nothing to do with philosophy."[27] Therefore, D&G hold that "it does no credit to philosophy for it to present itself as a new Athens by falling back on Universals of communication that would provide rules for an imaginary mastery of the markets and the media [another illusion of] (intersubjective idealism)" (7). In addition to the fact that such a conception of philosophy as a new Athens rests on a mistaken conception of what ancient Athens was all about, namely that philosophy as a Greek thing would be an attempt at discovering the golden middle of opinions, to seek to revive in contemporary philosophy ancient philosophy in such a way amounts to nothing less than raising an opinion to the level of a universal.[28] Undoubtedly, philosophy is something essentially Greek, but that does not make it into a universal that could, or should, be reactualized in the shape of a new Athens. The only way to be faithful to philosophy's origin in Greece is to get over it precisely by doing today what the Greeks did then, that is, creating new concepts. In distinction from the constitution of universals, "every creation is singular, and the concept as a specifically philosophical creation is always a singularity. The first principle of philosophy is that Universals explain nothing but must themselves be explained" (7).

So, if the "well-defined occupation or precise activity" (ibid.) of the philosopher is the creation of concepts—rather than being engaged in contemplation, reflection, and communication, which are no "more than opinions held about thought at a particular time and in a particular civilization" (37), rather than, in fact, what D&G call "the three figures of philosophy" (92), which are its scientific or religious misconceptions, namely, the construction of philosophy as doing science and thus being involved in the cognition of things, and rather than, finally, as a long tradition has held, a search "to know oneself, to learn to think, to act as if nothing were self-evident—wondering, 'wondering that there is being'" (7)—how, then, does one have to understand "creation" here?

As we have already seen, creation is not a forming, inventing, or fabricating. If it is none of these, it is above all because, according to D&G, to create is "the highest power of thought" (62). Now, from the context in which D&G speak about creation one may perhaps get the impression that creation is the defining power of thought as philosophical thought and that philosophical thought is the prime if not sole holder of this power. But that impression is not correct. Although this highest power of thought is in philosophy the origin of the creation of concepts, this same power is in the two other forms of thought—the sciences and the arts—the source of "the other creative Ideas that are not concepts . . . which have their own history and becoming and . . . their own variable relationships with one another and with philosophy" (8). Philosophy thus has no exclusive property right to creativity, and the activity of creating cannot be illuminated through the creation of concepts alone. D&G write: "The exclusive right of concept creation secures a function for philosophy, but it does not give it any preeminence or privilege since there are other ways of thinking and creating, other modes of ideation that, like scientific thought, do not have to pass through concepts. We always come back to the question of the use of this activity of creating concepts, in its difference from scientific or artistic activity" (ibid).

In any event, if philosophy is "knowledge through pure concepts" (7), such knowledge through pure concepts implies the creation, or "construction," of concepts within a "milieu," which is required for concepts to accomplish the immediate, or speedy, totalization of their components and, hence, also has to be characterized in itself by "fluidity" (36). This "indivisible milieu" is none other than the plane on which the concepts are created and "distributed without breaking up its continuity or integrity" (ibid.). Even though the term "milieu" comes from the Latin *medius*, middle, it has here to be understood, first and foremost, as the medium, the background, the setting, if not actually an opening (D&G also speak of the plane as an "absolute horizon" [ibid.]) within which concepts are created.[29] Now, if D&G hold that this milieu is indivisible and that the concepts that come to populate it do not split it up, it is intimated that the milieu or plane in question has something of a whole. As we have already seen, concepts are the dynamic totalities of their components. As we will see in a moment, in conceiving the plane on which concept creation takes place, D&G, all things considered, comply with the Socratic formal and logical requirement of the whole (*holon*), that is, of thinking according to the whole—*kath-holou*.[30]

Concepts are created "in an intuition specific to them: a field, a plane, and a ground that must not be confused with them but that shelters [*abrite*, houses] their seeds and the [conceptual] personae who cultivate them. Constructivism requires every creation to be a construction on a plane that gives it an autonomous existence" (7). Philosophy as construction, or creation, of concepts implies "the qualitatively different complementary" aspect of "the laying out of a plane," of instituting what D&G call "the plane of immanence" on which the concepts are created and, subsequently, come to populate (36).[31] Now the institution of the plane of immanence is described as "a section [*coupe*] of chaos [that] acts like a sieve" (42). In selectively choosing these components, the aim of this plane is "to ward off [*conjurer*]" chaos (51). This is expressed even more forcefully in the "Conclusion" to the book where D&G say, while referring to the arts, that "it is always a matter of defeating chaos by a secant plane that crosses it" (203). Here, at the end of the book, it is also made quite explicit that all three forms of thought—philosophy, the sciences, and the arts—are involved in a "*struggle against chaos*" (ibid.). They ask, indeed, "what would *thinking* be if it did not constantly confront chaos?" (208). Chaos, they claim, "has three daughters, depending on the plane that cuts through it: these are the *Chaoids*—art, science, and philosophy—as forms of thought or creation. We call *Chaoids* the realities produced on the planes that cut through the chaos in different ways" (208). The creation effectuated by the three forms of thought is thus intrinsically understood as a struggle in a violent confrontation with chaos, that is, the state of indistinction, undifferentiatedness, disorder, or mere multiplicity. In fact, the stakes of this confrontation, which will become more concrete when, a bit later, we take up the question of opinion, are survival itself. This becomes explicit at the moment when, at the end of the book, the planes that all three forms of thought drive through chaos are characterized as "rafts": philosophy, the sciences, and the arts "are the three planes, the rafts on which the brain plunges into and confronts chaos" (210). But this passage, which calls all three forms of thought by the name "Chaoids"—a name that resonates with so many Hesiodian mythical figures—also suggests that not only philosophy but also the arts and the sciences have a definitely Greek origin. This point is made again when it is said that with philosophy, science, and the arts "thrice victorious I have crossed the Acheron" and returned from "the land of the dead" (202). For the moment, however, I will limit myself primarily to philosophy's struggle with "the chaos as undifferentiated abyss or ocean of dissemblance" (207). A first hint at how to understand chaos is thus already provided.

Chaos is an unarticulated multiplicity. It contains the entirety of "all possible particles" (118), but these elements lack any form of connection. Chaos is a state of a complete lack of order and organization of its elements. But it "is not an inert or stationary state, nor is it a chance mixture" (42). Chaos is characterized by "infinite movements and speeds" (ibid.). If chaos is not a state of indeterminacy of its elements, it is precisely because chaos "makes chaotic (*chaotise*) and undoes every consistency in the infinite" (ibid.). Indeed, "chaos is characterized less by the absence of determinations than by the infinite speed with which they take shape and vanish. This is not a movement from one determination to the other but, on the contrary, the impossibility of a connection between them, since one does not appear without the other having already disappeared, and one appears as disappearance when the other disappears as outline" (ibid.). In sum, chaos is a highly dynamic state in which the elements are in a process of emerging as determinate, or discrete elements while at the same time disappearing again at infinite speed without ever gaining any consistency. Nothing resembles itself in this state, that is, no-thing emerges here as having an identity, and no connections between elements come into being. Now, at the beginning of the chapter on "Functives and Concepts," that is, the chapter on the "difference between science and philosophy" (117), a reference to Ilya Prigogine and Isabelle Stengers's work shows the indebtedness of D&G's conception to chaos theory. Although I wonder whether Hesiod and Nietzsche are not the primary sources of their understanding of chaos, the reference to both authors seems to introduce an additional aspect of what constitutes chaos. Even at the risk of some redundancy I need to quote a longer passage in its entirety: "Chaos is defined not so much by its disorder as by the infinite speed with which every form taking shape in it vanishes. It is a void that is not a nothingness but a *virtual*, containing all possible particles and drawing out all possible forms, which spring up only to disappear immediately, without consistency of reference, without consequence. Chaos is an infinite speed of birth and disappearance" (118). What is important in this passage is the notion that chaos is a virtual in that it contains all possible particles and forms. Chaos is the medium, as it were, in which what is virtual awaits its actualization in the three irreducible forms of thought along with their respective elements: "*plane of immanence of philosophy, plane of composition of art, plane of reference or coordination of science; form of concept, force of sensation, function of knowledge; concepts and conceptual personae, sensations and aesthetic figures, figures and partial observers*" (216). Not unlike the field of forces manifested by the Higgs boson which, according to the Standard Model, is comparable to a kind of molasses that permeates space, and prevents the elementary forms of matter from just zooming around at the speed of light by providing them with the mass necessary for there to be atoms, and hence matter, the planes that cut through chaos actualize it in the different shapes of the concepts, functives, and percepts/affects through which the particles and forms of chaos become imbued with reality. Furthermore, since chaos contains all possible particles and forms only in a virtual form, their actualization is not one of possibilities, that is, of preformed or anticipatable elements and forms, but, rather, of events that themselves are a function of the intervention of the plane in chaos.

To cut through the mess of chaos with a plane philosophy must plunge (*plonger,* to dive) into it. In other words, the plane of immanence partakes in chaos in that its objective is not only to bring about consistency but also to acquire that consistency "without losing the infinite into which thought [as philosophical thought] plunges" (42). Undoubtedly, the term "plunge" resonates with the sympathy that is constitutive of intuition according to Bergson. But unlike Bergson's "indivisible apprehension" of the intuition of something from within, chaos is not apprehended absolutely, since the totalization that the plane of immanence effectuates in chaos is selective (and, hence, also infinitely repeatable in always different ways). If, furthermore, D&G assert that the consistency that the plane accomplishes does not surrender infinity, the difference with respect to Bergson is that for the latter infinity is an attribute of science's effort to circumscribe an object from outside in an endless task.[32] As D&G remark, what philosophy accomplishes with respect to chaos "is very different from the problem of science, which seeks to provide chaos with reference points, on condition of renouncing infinite movements and speeds and of carrying out a limitation of speed first of all" (42). I already mentioned the "fantastic *slowing down*" (118) that reference in the sciences performs, whose approach, in Bergsonian terms, is through symbols or, in D&G's terms, through functives. Terminologically speaking, the difference in question between the three modes of thought is a difference between a plane of immanence characterized by consistency, a plane whose prime trait is referentiality, and another that consists of composition (the arts). Concerning the arts' way of struggling with chaos and its movements of infinite speed, they are said to "pass through the finite in order to rediscover, to restore the infinite" (197) and "to render it sensory" (205). Now, let us remind ourselves that the plane that cuts a section through chaos has been compared to a sieve, which means simply that the plane, whatever its nature, does not embrace all of chaos's elements and speeds since otherwise it would be indistinguishable from chaos itself (49). As a sieve a plane is necessarily selective.

In *What Is Philosophy?* D&G argue forcefully that "it is essential not to confuse the plane of immanence and the concepts that occupy it": between both there is a "difference in nature" (39)—a difference in kind, rather than one of degree. Let us remind ourselves that the conception of the "plane of immanence" consists in the intuition of the indivisible milieu of "a powerful Whole that, while remaining open, is not fragmented [like the concepts]: an unlimited One-All (*Un-Tout*), an 'Omnitudo,' that includes all the concepts on one and the same plane" (35). Both terms, "intuition" and "One-All," need elucidation. So, first, a word on the notion of intuition: rather than referring to a sixth sense or some sort of mystical apprehension, intuition here has to be understood primarily from the Latin verb *intuire,* which means to look at, upon, or toward, and, when said of the mind, to regard, observe, contemplate, consider, give attention, and so forth. In German philosophy, intuition is thus generally translated as "*Anschauung,*" though the Latin is used as well, by Nietzsche for instance. Undoubtedly, D&G's use of the term is indebted to Bergson's understanding of it in *Introduction to Metaphysics.* For Bergson, intuition is, first of all, a methodical concept intent on overcoming the two antagonistic trends in modern philosophy of idealism and realism in which the "consciousness we have of our own self in its continual flux" becomes the model for representing reality no longer understood as made up of fixed things or stable states of affairs but as mobility and becoming.[33] Intuition is, as already said, not some lofty mystic experience, since, when lifted from the experience of myself to the real, it demands a considerable effort in that it goes against the grain of our common experience. Indeed, as Bergson makes amply clear, in intuition "the mind has to do violence to itself."[34] Intuition which, in contrast to common sense, and even the sciences, provides "an internal and metaphysical knowledge of the real," stands in opposition to analysis (and, hence, is not a kind of synthesis which itself is of the order of a reconstruction following the analytical break up of a thing, or experience).[35] Rather, it is an immediate (sudden, that is, not by way of consecutive perceptions) and concrete awareness, in advance of the classical divide between the sensory and the intellectual, of something in its entirety such as, for instance, the apprehension of my body from within.[36] But, given the preeminence of Nietzschean thought in *What Is Philosophy?,* I also wish to follow up on the Nietzschean resonances of the notion of intuition in the present context. It is, as I said, an intuition in advance, as it were, of concept creation, an immediate and concrete apprehension of the One-All that concepts will serve to flesh out.

One of the reasons why I highlight the Nietzschean component in D&G's understanding of the concept of intuition is that, like Nietzsche, D&G think of the essence of philosophy primarily from its pre-Socratic instantiation. For both Nietzsche and D&G, what these early Greek thinkers accomplished was nothing less than an understanding of reality to be in constant and continuous flux rather than made of stable and discrete things or states of affairs that could be understood either by Ideas or concepts in the classical sense. If D&G, in the same way as Nietzsche, think philosophy from the pre-Socratics, it is because from the beginning they themselves have been anti-Platonists, and pre-Socratic thought already, and in advance, upended the hierarchies of values that Platonism was to establish and that, subsequently, came to dominate Western philosophical thought. For D&G, the pre-Socratics were thus also already involved in a kind of intuition of the real that for Bergson is the characteristic of modern philosophical thought alone as a thought that reverses the Platonic valorization of the ideas over the soul, the immutable over the mobile, the stable over the instable and that "thus tends, like modern science, and even more so than modern science, to advance in an opposite direction [*en sens inverse*] to ancient thought."[37] It is in this context as well that one can grasp what philosophy is for D&G, both in the Greek sense and in the sense of what they have sought to live up to in their own doing of philosophy. Philosophy is genuine philosophy only if it is the reverse of an ontology of Being, that is, in Kathrin Thiele's words, an "ontology of becoming," and if, without exception, the categorical apparatus to think becoming remains in its entirety true to the dynamic nature of the real.[38]

To return to the question of the plane of immanence, let us bear in mind that "plane" (in French, "plan") in the sense of a flat or level surface comes from the Latin *planum,* meaning level ground, as well as a plain, that is, a flat area of land. Consistent with my attempt to retranslate D&G's technical terms into more traditional philosophical terms, I hold that their notion of "plane" echoes "the plain of Truth" (*aletheias idein pedion*), or the hyperouranian "meadow," of which Plato speaks in the *Phaedrus* (248b–c), and on which "true being," that is, the ideas, can be beheld. What mainly distinguishes Plato's plain of truth from the plane of immanence is, first, that the former is located beyond not only the heavens but also the earth, whereas the plane of immanence cuts through both, and, second, that the plane of immanence is populated not by ideas per se but by "philosophical Ideas," in short, concepts. Now, as already indicated, the plane of immanence also consists of the intuition of a Whole, or One-All. To grasp how this is to be understood, a brief digression through "Philosophy During the Tragic Age of the Greeks" is warranted—a text that *What Is Philosophy?* features as one of its references—where Nietzsche argues that the origin of philosophy in Greece is tied to a "metaphysical dogma [*Glaubenssatz*], which had its origin in a mystic intuition."[39] Although I said before that there is no mystical experience involved in intuition, Nietzsche's qualification of the term seems to suggest otherwise. Indeed, the first Greek philosopher, that is, Thales, still seems to partake "in the company of religious and superstitious people," and this, it seems, explains why Nietzsche talks about mysticism.[40] But what Nietzsche subsequently offers concerning this intuition seems to belie all negative connotations of the term since this very intuition, according to Nietzsche, already "takes him out of this company."[41] Furthermore, the intuition that makes Thales the first philosopher is at the same time an intuition by which "he went beyond the scientific."[42] In Deleuzian and Guattarian terms, Thales is thus the first genuine philosopher, no longer a sage, nor a scientist, but one who seeks knowledge through pure concept creation. What, then, according to Nietzsche, is the constitutive intuition that from the start distinguishes philosophy from science and religion, "which, together with the ever renewed endeavours to express it better, *we find in all philosophies*" (emphasis mine)?[43] This claim is echoed by D&G when they invoke "the grandiose Leibnizian or Bergsonian perspective that every philosophy depends upon an intuition that its concepts constantly develop through slight differences of intensity . . . [and that] is thought of as the envelopment of infinite movements of thought that constantly pass through a plane of immanence" (40). "Water" is the concept by means of which Thales already sought to articulate the unity of Being that he beheld. Nietzsche writes: "Thales saw the Unity of the 'Existent' [*die Einheit des Seienden*], and when he wanted to communicate this idea he talked of water."[44] Even if Thales's intuition, according to Nietzsche, proceeds "without figure and fable," it is not the proposition "that water [or, for that matter, air, the undetermined, fire, and so forth] is the origin and motherwomb of all things" but "the proposition: *Everything is one!*" Although the idea that everything is One is found "only in the chrysalis state [*im Zustande der Verpuppung*]" in the assumption that water is the source of everything, it is this idea, or intuition, that makes Thales the first philosopher.[45] Now, I wish to contend that what D&G call the "plane of immanence" is, all things considered, another name for this intuition through which, in Nietzsche's words, "the philosopher tries to make the totalchord [*Gesamtklang*] of the universe reecho within himself and then to project it into concepts outside himself [*und ihn aus sich herauszustellen in Begriffen*]."[46] The plane of immanence, or the One-All, that philosophy produces by cutting through chaos is also referred to by D&G as "the great panic Plane" (224n14)—a reference to Friedrich Hölderlin that evidences, furthermore, that the intuition of the One-All that forms the plane in question corresponds to the Greek notion of *hen kai pan*, an expression that the German Idealists used in a prominent fashion in their interpretation of Spinoza's thought[47]—and for D&G, as seen, this is the plane in which concept creation occurs in view of problems to be solved.

Since D&G speak of "the One-All of the plane of immanence" (38), stating that "every plane of immanence is a One-All" (50), the plane must inevitably be understood from the proposition that everything is one. Still, there are also differences that must be noted. In spite of D&G's suggestion at the beginning of *What Is Philosophy?* that, apart from the creation of concepts, the tracing of a plane of immanence is also a specific accomplishment of philosophy, such tracing is not the exclusive property of philosophy. For D&G, first of all, all types of thought—the sciences, philosophy, and the arts—are said to operate on planes. Second, since the plane of immanence that cuts through chaos functions like a sieve and is thus selective, the intuition of the One-All that it represents is always only a singular all-embracing One, whatever its force may be, and, consequently, susceptible to creative replacement. Third, the planes in question are of the order of a negative within all three forms of thought, or disciplines. Through its plane each discipline is "in an essential relation with the No that concerns it" (218): with nonphilosophy in the case of philosophy, nonscience in the case of science, and with nonart in the case of art. D&G write: "The plane of philosophy is prephilosophical insofar as we consider it in itself independently of the concepts that come to occupy it, but nonphilosophy is found where the plane confronts chaos. *Philosophy needs a nonphilosophy that comprehends it; it needs a nonphilosophical comprehension just as art needs nonart and science needs nonscience*" (ibid.).[48] Only later will I draw out the full implications of these statements when I address the question of how the three disciplines, or forms of thought, relate to one another, and take up again the question posed at the beginning concerning the role of philosophy in the differentiations of the three forms of thought. For the time being, I want to retain only the contention that the plane on which all three forms operate is with respect to each discipline a No insofar as it is considered in itself independently of what comes to occupy it, that is, first and foremost, insofar as the plane confronts chaos. All three disciplines have in common the plane that takes on chaos, and they become what they specifically are only insofar as they populate the plane with concepts, functives, or percepts respectively. I quote: "The three routes are specific, each as direct as the others, and they are distinguished by the nature of the plane and by what occupies it. Thinking is thought through concepts, or functions, or sensations and no one of these thoughts is better than another, or more fully, completely, or synthetically 'thought' " (198).

To return, then, to the case of philosophy, because the plane of immanence that it presupposes is "pre-philosophical and does not immediately take effect with concepts, it implies a sort of groping experimentation and its layout resorts to measures that are not very respectable, rational, or reasonable" (41). This is obviously in reference to D&G's contention that for all philosophical concept-creation a certain pre-conceptual, or pre-rational, intuition of a One-All by which a plane is instituted through an act distinct from the creation of concepts is indispensable, an intuition that provides the ground that concepts subsequently come to populate, which is philosophy's defining operation. If the plane of immanence is not philosophical from the start but grounded in a prephilosophical intuition, is it not also because, furthermore, the plane in question is "the nonthought within thought" (59)? Although philosophy presupposes the plane of immanence, "it is laid out as presupposed and not because it preexists without being laid out" (78). If in philosophy the plane of immanence is the nonphilosophical, not yet philosophical intuition of "the horizon of the events" (36), that is, the created concepts that themselves are what is specifically philosophical, it is also the case that the concepts affect the plane that "becomes philosophical only through the effect of the concept. Although the plane is presupposed by philosophy, it is nonetheless instituted by it and it unfolds in a philosophical relationship with the nonphilosophical" (93). Therefore, the emergence of philosophy in Greece is not only tied to the creation of concepts but also linked with the instauration of a specifically philosophical, or, as we will see, radically immanent, plane.

At this juncture let me bring up again D&G's contention that the plane of immanence "constitutes the absolute ground of philosophy, its earth or [its] deterritorialization, the foundation on which it creates its concepts" (41). The very idea of a plane of immanence calls upon the Earth as a foundation. If philosophy is an essentially Greek thing, it is because of the Earth, which the Greeks conceived, as we have already seen D&G to hold, as the deterritorialized par excellence and as something that they wrenched from mother earth, detaching from all blood and soil connotations. Is it not this very concern with the Earth, that is, philosophy's intrinsically geophilosophical nature, that presupposes the drawing of a still pre-philosophical plane of immanence through chaos that deterritorializes the mythical Gaia and makes this plane into the Earth *of* philosophy? Wrested from Gaia, the Earth is freed into an immanence with itself. The Earth as the ground, the foundation of philosophy, is an Earth that is freed from Nativeness, that is, autochthonous in a new sense, and that knows no hierarchy, hegemony, domination, or, philosophically speaking, transcendence. In this sense, this Earth of philosophy is Greek. But since the prephilosophical intuition that cuts through chaos, and according to which All is One, is also always singular, the Earth of philosophy, as the deterritorialized par excellence, will always be singular as well, and plural in its very immanence. The plane of immanence, then, is within thought the equivalent of the political earth, or public place, in which Greek life unfolds. And if the creation of concepts, together with the plane on which it takes place, represents the second characteristic of philosophy as a Greek thing, it is also to be thought devolving directly from this very concern with the earth.

6

Liberating Opinion

Before I take up the third feature of philosophy, the one that concerns opinion, to show that it too is intimately tied to D&G's understanding of philosophy as in essence geophilosophical, I would like to circle back to the notion of creation with the second feature of philosophy in mind. From what we have seen, creation is "to make something" [*c'est faire quelque chose,* it is doing something in the first place] (7). In *Negotiations,* as opposed to reactively taking refuge in reflection defined as being always about something pregiven, creation is said to "make [the] move," that is, the movement of unblocking thought insofar as it is seen to be situated in the between of origins and ends.[1] More specifically, creation is a movement or doing through which something that has an autonomous existence (even though virtual seeds of it are to be found, or, in retrospect, will have been found, in the intuited plane that is sliced through chaos) is wrested (and set free) in a violent, creative move from chaos in which everything turns in infinite speed into something else, never enjoying any autonomy whatsoever, and that, furthermore, is irreducibly singular. As D&G contend, an index for the singularity of concepts, that is, for their createdness or constructedness, is that "concepts are and remain signed: Aristotle's substance, Descartes' cogito, Leibniz's monad, Kant's condition, Schelling's power, Bergson's duration" (7). But singular names chosen for concepts are not only witness to their createdness; they also testify to a specifically philosophical form of taste that guides their creation. D&G write:

> Some concepts must be indicated by an extraordinary and sometimes even barbarous or shocking word, whereas others make do with an ordinary, everyday word that is filled with harmonics so distant that it risks being imperceptible to a nonphilosophical ear. Some concepts call for archaisms, and others for neologisms, shot through with almost crazy etymological exercises. . . . In each case there must be a strange necessity for these words and for their choice, like an element of style. The concept's baptism calls for a specifically philosophical taste that proceeds with violence or by insinuation and constitutes a philosophical language—not just a vocabulary but a syntax that attains the sublime or a great beauty. (7–8)

I will dwell for a moment on this question of a specifically philosophical taste. And I wish to do this, first, by way of another digression to Nietzsche's essay from 1873. Since Nietzsche does not yet radically distinguish between the philosophical genius and the sage, he can resort to the etymological roots of the word "sage" to highlight a specific characteristic of the philosopher, especially in light of what distinguishes him from the man of science. Nietzsche writes: "The Greek word which designates the Sage belongs etymologically to *sapio,* I taste, *sapiens,* the tasting one, *sisyphos,* the man of the most delicate taste; the peculiar art of the philosopher therefore consists, according to the opinion of the people, in a delicate selective judgment by taste, by discernment, by significant differentiation."[2] Indeed, this Nietzschean conception of the philosopher, in particular of the first Greek philosophers, that is, also of philosophy as a Greek thing, has again stood sponsor, I believe, for what D&G will establish about philosophical taste in the following.

As we have seen, a concept's consistency is accomplished by the partial overlapping of the multiple but finite number of its components that thus become linked through zones, thresholds, and bridges that themselves provide the passages through which the "conceptual point" (20) or "point of condensation" (58) can fly at more or less infinite speed and totalize them at one blow. In conformity with what we have learned about the concept of survey, such totalization of all the components of a concept by the concept that skims over them accomplishes its primary self-consciousness, or rather self-referentiality. The intelligibility of concepts is not logical, and, since they have no referent, their intelligibility is not a function of a transcendental logic either. By contrast, their intelligibility seems to be constituted by a transcendental aesthetic of some sort. As suggested by the spatial or territorial metaphors and the metaphors of time (as well as the more or less infinite speed with which they connect, movement being intimately tied to time since Aristotle) to which D&G resort to describe how the components of concepts are held together and bring forth their self-referentiality, concepts (as well as the relations between concepts) have, as they insist on several occasions, something sensible about them.[3] Now, as the reference to a specifically philosophical taste shows, a specifically philosophical kind of aesthetic judgment is involved in the creation of concepts. In Chapter 3 on the "Conceptual Personae," after having recalled that philosophy is constituted by three elements—the tracing of the plane of immanence, the invention of the conceptual personae, and the creation of the concepts—D&G note that for these three elements, which cannot be deduced from one another, to be coadapted "[a] whole 'taste' is needed here" (77). As the following quotation demonstrates, the allusion to Kant's three Critiques and their respective powers of the mind is obvious:

> The philosophical faculty of coadaptation, which also regulates the creation of concepts, is called *taste.* If the laying-out of the plane is called Reason, the invention of personae Imagination, and the creation of concepts Understanding, then taste appears as the triple faculty of the still-undetermined concept, of the persona still in limbo, and of the still-transparent plane. That is why it is necessary to create, invent, and lay out, while taste is like the rule of correspondence of the three instances that are different in kind. (Ibid.)

As regards the creation of concepts, "philosophical taste neither replaces creation nor restrains it. On the contrary, the creation of concepts calls for a taste that modulates it" (78). More precisely, "what appears as philosophical taste in every case is love of the well-made concept," "well-made" meaning "a sort of modulation in which conceptual activity has no limit in itself [as would be the case if concepts were ready made in advance] but only in the other two limitless activities," that is, the tracing of the plane of immanence and the invention of the conceptual personae (77). To link the creation of concepts to taste is indispensable not only if they are to be well-made concepts, but also, and especially, if concepts are to be singular creations that have their own specific beauty or sublimity—though not works of art, which is the other form of thought distinct from philosophy and the sciences. Finally, if philosophical taste is the "being-potential [*être-en-puissance*] of the concept," this is further evidence of the fact that "it is certainly not for 'rational or reasonable' reasons that a particular concept is created or a particular component chosen" (78). Modulated by taste, the creation of concepts thus provides additional demonstration of the nonrational, and nonscientific, intelligibility of conceptual and philosophical thought. That Nietzsche has from the beginning inflected all the references to Kant's three powers of the mind is made manifest when D&G write in conclusion that "Nietzsche sensed this relationship of the creation of concepts with a specifically philosophical taste, and if the philosopher is he who creates concepts, it is thanks to a faculty of taste that is like an instinctive, almost animal *sapere*—a *Fiat* or a *Fatum* that gives each philosopher the right of access to certain problems, like an imprint on his name or an affinity from which his works flow" (78–79).

Now even though concepts are "dated, signed, and baptized, they have their own way of not dying while remaining subject to constraints of renewal, replacement, and mutation that give philosophy a history as well as a turbulent geography, each moment and place of which is preserved (but in time) and that passes (but outside time)" (8). The very singularity of concepts, that which, precisely, would seem to make them ephemeral constructs, is what provides philosophy with both a history and a geography, that is, an immortality in time through its transformations and changes in its specific geographical settings.[4] But this history and geography of philosophy also impose the question of what it is that provides the unity of philosophical thought, and, in particular, "why, through what necessity, and for what use must concepts, and always new concepts, be created? And in order to do what?" (8–9). The question is all the more urgent given that D&G neither buy into the traditional responses to this question nor take seriously, as we have already seen, the claim that philosophy is at its end. At the same time, Deleuze points to the complexity of a possible answer to the above question when he asserts in *Dialogues II* that, because philosophy is not an ultimate discipline, "there is no need for philosophy," that, therefore, philosophy is "necessarily produced" by artworks, for example, only where artistic activity "gives rise to its line of deterritorialization," and, finally, that to do philosophy one must "get out of philosophy . . . so as to be able to produce it from outside."[5]

D&G's answer to these questions hinges partially on what they construe as the third characteristic of philosophy that makes it an essentially Greek thing. But before I address this feature, it may be appropriate to recapitulate the first two characteristics. In the chapter on "The Plane of Immanence," D&G note that "to the question 'Can or must philosophy be regarded as Greek?' a first answer seemed to be that the Greek city actually appears as the new society of 'friends,' with all the ambiguities of the word. Jean-Pierre Vernant adds a second answer: the Greeks were the first to conceive of a strict immanence of Order to a cosmic milieu that sections chaos in the form of a plane" (43). The second characteristic that makes Greece the origin of philosophy is the Greeks' conception of the strict immanence, that is, without transcendence of any kind, of the cosmic milieu. As the pages in Vernant's study to which they refer clearly indicate, this orderly cosmic milieu is conceived after the "order and the law whose success in the city had made the human world a cosmos," or, in D&G's terms, an Earth.[6] As should have become clear already, D&G understand Greek philosophy primarily from the Ionian philosophy of nature. As Vernant remarks, the Ionian " 'natural philosophers' deliberately ignored the domain of religion." For them "nothing existed that was not nature, *physis* . . . which excluded the very notion of anything supernatural."[7] It is this "desacralization of knowledge" by pre-Socratic thought, "the advent of a kind of thought foreign to religion," that D&G have in mind when they characterize Greek philosophy as a conception of a strict immanence.[8]

As the notion of a plane that sections chaos indicates, this second characteristic of philosophy is the plane of immanence that the creation of concepts entails. D&G add: "If we call such a plane-sieve Logos, the logos is far from being like simple 'reason' (as when one says the world is rational). Reason is only a concept, and a very impoverished concept for defining the plane and the movements that pass through it. In short, the first philosophers are those who institute a plane of immanence like a sieve stretched over the chaos" (43). Rather than a concept in Greek thought, logos, then, is a pre-conceptual, indeed, pre-philosophical intuition that by slicing through chaos gathers it into a whole, into a "One-All" to be beheld in intuition, in, or on, whose plane concepts are created. And if logos is precisely a strictly immanent plane of chaos, then the philosophers

> contrast with sages, who are religious personae, priests, because they conceive of the institution of an always transcendent order imposed from outside by a great despot or by one god higher than the others, inspired by Eris, pursuing wars that go beyond any agon and hatreds that object in advance to the trials of rivalry. Whenever there is transcendence, vertical Being, imperial State in the sky or on the earth, there is religion; and there is Philosophy whenever there is immanence. (Ibid.)

In short, the plane of immanence that the Greek thinkers trace through chaos is a plane that is rigorously a-mythical and a-religious, absolutely a-theist. Philosophy is a Greek thing only when philosophy rejects transcendence in every form, and above all the figures of deities, idols, or one God. Only such thought of radical immanence can truly co-adapt to a society of friends, the first condition for philosophy. D&G write: "Perhaps these two possible determinations of philosophy as Greek are profoundly linked. Only friends can set out a plane of immanence as a ground from which idols have been cleared" (ibid.). While it is true that the first philosophers (Empedocles, the thinker of *philia,* for example) may still look like priests and may "borrow the sage's mask" (ibid.)—as we have noted, in another reference to Nietzsche—they "carry out a vast diversion of wisdom; they place it at the service of pure immanence. They replace genealogy with a geology" (44). Insofar as it drives a plane of immanence through chaos, philosophy as the creation of concepts—whose pre-philosophical and fully immanent plane consists of two sides: "one determinable as Physis inasmuch as it endows Being with a substance, and the other as Nous inasmuch as it gives an image to thought" (ibid.)—thus rests on an intuition of the whole, of the One-All, as the articulation of logos *and* earth: geo-logy. Geophilosophy, literally, is a geology, that is, a logos, a discourse, or a thinking of the earth—geo-logy.

Now, to gauge the full meaning of this second characteristic of philosophy, and thus of what the Greek contribution amounts to, in short, of what philosophy as a *Greek* thing ultimately signifies, I need to evoke a motif in D&G's thought that is absolutely crucial to understanding the so-called "Greek miracle." This is a motif raised in the context of their elaboration on the conceptual personae, namely, the motif of "believing in this world" (75). In relation to today's situation, D&G submit that "it may be that believing in this world, in this life, becomes our most difficult task, or the task of a mode of existence still to be discovered on our plane of immanence today. This is the empiricist conversion (we have so many reasons not to believe in the human world; we have lost the world, worse than a fiancée or a god)" (ibid.). The problem is no longer whether God exists or not; on the new plane on which we exist the problem is an altogether different one. The problem "now concerns the one who believes in the world," not so much "in the existence of the world [as] in its possibilities of movements and intensities, so as once again to give birth to new modes of existence, closer to animals and rocks" (74–75). To define philosophy as a Greek thing, in which a strictly immanent plane cuts through the chaos on which concepts can be created, is to define it in terms of a belief in this world, in this earth—echoing Zarathustra's exclamation: "we certainly do not want to enter into the kingdom of heaven: we have become men, *so we want the kingdom of earth.*"[9] As one can glean from Chapter 4 on "Geophilosophy," the philosophical creation of concepts as understood by D&G is meaningful exclusively within the frame of such an affirmation of the world, or the earth, in all its present presence. It rests on an unconditional affirmation of this world, or this earth, and its immanent and virtual possibilities. As geophilosophy, philosophy is Greek and witness to a belief in this and no other world, and it is, therefore, for this reason, that in *What Is Philosophy?* D&G are so concerned with philosophy's Greek origins.[10]

Even though D&G will only explicitly refer to a third characteristic of philosophy as in essence a Greek thing in chapter 3, I wish to frame this third determination by the question raised in the "Introduction" concerning the use of philosophy. To answer this question they return to the question of the friend, or lover, who as a claimant necessarily has rivals. They write: "If we really want to say that philosophy originates with the Greeks, it is because the city, unlike the empire or state, invents the agon as the rule of a society of 'friends,' of the community of free men as rivals (citizens)" (9). But as "the invariable situation described by Plato" shows, such invention of a milieu of contest would seem to require one to be able to judge the validity of the competing claims, especially in the domain of politics "where, according to Plato, anyone can lay claim to anything in Athenian democracy" (ibid.). Rivalry thus calls for standards to judge the rivals, the claimants, and the claims they make. Plato sought to answer this challenge with "the Ideas as philosophical concepts" (ibid.), and thus to establish the necessity and usefulness of philosophy. But as the battle between the philosopher and the sophist demonstrate, the distinction between the true and the false friend, between the concept and the simulacrum, is part of the "Platonic theater" (10) and remains a constant task. The search for criteria for judging the truth of claims made in a milieu where everyone can profess an opinion does not find any final solution. The search for a standard is no less a task in our time, D&G note, wherein "philosophy has encountered many new rivals" (ibid.). Among such rivals are the sciences and all the disciplines of communication, in other words, computer science, marketing, design, and advertising. They all have taken hold of the concept, which now "has become the set of product displays" (ibid.). "But," D&G continue, "the more philosophy comes up against shameless and inane rivals and encounters them at its very core, the more it feels driven to fulfill the task of creating concepts that are aerolites rather than commercial products. It gets the giggles, which wipe away its tears. So, the question of philosophy is the singular point where concept and creation are related to each other" (11). Indeed, if the search for a standard for judging competing claims does not result in a definite and satisfactory answer, and if philosophy is in essence the creation of concepts, is it not because the concept as a philosophical idea accomplishes something other than just a standard against which to measure competing claims? If this is the case, the question of philosophy, namely, the question about its utility, needs to be revisited. The necessity of the creation of concepts, as distinct from the functives of the sciences and the percepts of the arts, may not lie with any usefulness, at least not in a narrow sense, but may have to be retraced to what D&G call "the nature of the concept as philosophical reality" (ibid.).

Let us, then, proceed to the third characteristic of philosophy that causes it to be a Greek thing, as well. And again we will have to ask, even though it would seem that in this particular case the question is more difficult to answer, to what extent it, too, presupposes a conception of earth as an autonomous and entirely immanent reality. The distinction between philosophical and scientific problems provides the context in which this third characteristic is introduced. Following Emile Bréhier who, in "La notion de problème en philosophie," had already argued that problems always presuppose a "meta-problematic" and that "the danger of philosophy is to distort the original character of its own problems by linking them to a meta-problematic that is not appropriate to them," D&G call to mind again that "since concepts are not propositional, they cannot refer to problems concerning the extensional conditions of propositions assimilable to those of science" (79).[11] Concepts generate only solutions, or contributions to solutions, to philosophical problems. D&G add:

> If we insist nonetheless on translating the philosophical concept into propositions, this can only be in the form of more-or-less plausible opinions without scientific value. But in this way we encounter a difficulty that the Greeks had already come up against. This is the third characteristic by which philosophy is thought of as something Greek: the Greek city puts forward the friend or rival as social relation, and it lays out a plane of immanence—but it also makes *free opinion* (*doxa*) prevail [*fait règner la* libre opinion] Philosophy must therefore extract from opinions a "knowledge" that transforms them but that is also distinct from science. (Ibid.; trans. mod.)

The key term here is "opinion," *free* opinion, that is, an opinion liberated from its constraints and limits qua opinion, in short, an opinion that is no longer measured by the yardstick of truth—for example, by the Platonic Idea—and that through this liberation acquires an unheard-of peculiar autonomy and is raised to infinity. Furthermore, the knowledge that philosophy is to extract from opinions that have an independence of their own can in no way be that of truth then, but must be of the order of such free opinions' inner consistency and self-relatedness. Considering the positive valuation that D&G accord to a politico-social space in which equals relate to equals and the immanence that such an order of a human cosmos accomplishes, in the passage in question they definitely make an unequivocal claim for the right to such free opinion. As something by which the Greeks distinguished themselves from the oriental empires, such freedom to have an opinion is something that D&G clearly hail as part of the "Greek miracle." The reign of free opinion in the polis is thus an unconditionally good thing, one more accomplishment of the Greek polis, especially since "opinion" seems not only to stress the singularity of the beliefs held but also to anticipate the concepts in the domain of philosophy. As D&G note, in the Greek sociopolitical milieu one of the three de facto conditions of philosophical thought is represented by "a taste for opinion inconceivable in an empire, a taste for the exchange of views, for conversation," that is, for one form of what Simmel had called "pure sociability," which they oppose to discussions that the philosopher abhors (88). Indeed, a society of more or less friendly rivals, claimants, or pretenders is one in which everyone has a right to his or her opinion, and thus one in which free opinion reigns, where opinions can be exchanged and conversed about without being contrasted to true opinions, or more generally to truth, that is, without anyone's opinion running the risk of being destroyed. As Simmel put it, "at the very moment a conversation becomes objective [*sachlich*], it is no longer sociable. Its teleological edge [*Spitze*] is inverted as soon as the discovery of a truth that, of course, can constitute its *content* becomes its very *purpose*."[12]

This third feature of philosophy would thus also be a necessary consequence of the geophilosophical nature of philosophy, of its involvement in the earth as a sociopolitical space. But to sustain this conclusion a series of possible difficulties have to be taken into account. As the citation in parentheses of the Greek word for opinion, namely *doxa*, that immediately follows the evocation of the "*free opinion*" that reigns in the Greek city seems to suggest, the Greeks, who, as Heidegger once put it, lived in discourse, also produced so much "babble [*Geschwätz*] that it required the total efforts of [both Plato and Aristotle] to be serious about the possibility of science."[13] No doubt, with this reference to *doxa*, opinion is qualified as frivolous. More importantly, however, the reference to *doxa* in this characterization of the third distinguishing feature of philosophy as Greek is also a reference to the criticism of opinion consistent throughout the whole history of philosophical thought, where it is regularly contrasted with truth, beginning with Parmenides, and with episteme or knowledge, since Plato and Aristotle. D&G not only acknowledge that much, but also, as the chapter on "Prospects and Concepts" especially seems to suggest, they fully underwrite philosophy's condemnation of *doxa*, even to the degree of sharply taking issue with those attempts in phenomenological thought to determine a legitimate place for and even fundamental function of opinion.

Yet, if the three characteristics by which philosophy became related to the Greek city are "the society of friends, the table of immanence, and the confrontation of opinions," to any positive valuation of opinion one might object, as D&G themselves do, "that Greek philosophers were always attacking *doxa* and contrasting it with an episteme as the only knowledge adequate to philosophy. But this is a mixed-up business, and philosophers, being only friends and not wise men, find it very difficult to give up *doxa*" (145). Indeed, an inner resistance by philosophy to altogether relinquishing *doxa* in the name of a knowledge worthy of philosophy is acknowledged here. In "Example 11" the point is made again, with the following addition: "Whether or not they were democrats, the Greeks did not so much oppose knowledge and opinion as fight over opinions, as confront and compete against each other in the element of pure opinion" (147). In other words, the traditional opposition between *doxa* and episteme is in reality, perhaps, not as clear cut when it comes to establishing what philosophy as a Greek thing consists in. Repeating again that philosophers are not sages and, consequently, do not possess the latter's knowledge (*savoir*), D&G write that "the philosophers lay claim to a knowledge that is distinct from the old wisdom and to an opinion that is distinct from that of the sophists" (228n9). As this footnote indicates, D&G refer here to Detienne's *The Masters of Truth in Archaic Greece,* which, I hold, is a crucial source for their positive valorization of *doxa* and their differentiation of two kinds of opinion. Indeed, after having shown that *Aletheia* is a religious symbol claimed by the sages and the inspired poets of mythical time, as well as by the later philosophico-religious sects, a first devaluation of *Aletheia* takes place with Simonides of Ceos, who turned poetry-making into a profession and composed poems for a fee. By his break away from the tradition of the inspired poets, "Simonides seems to be categorically rejecting the old religious concept of a poet, prophet of the Muses and master of *Aletheia.*"[14] Detienne writes: "To take its place, he recommended *to dokein, doxa.*"[15] This is also the first time that, according to Detienne, "*Aletheia* was directly opposed to *doxa,*" thus initiating an opposition and conflict that was to weigh in a decisive fashion on the whole history of philosophy in Greece insofar as the word came to be associated with the world of ambiguity, deceit, and precariousness and thus became the opposite of philosophical episteme in the fifth century.[16] Now, Simonides was, as Detienne remarks, "one of the first poets 'committed' to the city," followed later by the sophists and rhetoricians who further devalued *Aletheia* and continued the process of secularization.[17] His, and their, domain was "the political sphere, [that is,] the particular world of ambiguity."[18] Simonides's "insistence on the superiority of *doxa* over *Aletheia* does not result from the perspective defined by Parmenides," and *doxa* "does not mean opinion in the philosophical sense."[19] Understanding *doxa* from the verb *dokein,* which "is a technical term in the vocabulary of the polis, [a] verb used par excellence for political 'decision'," *doxa* refers to the kind of knowledge, the only one appropriate in the political sphere.[20] Detienne writes that by "clearly breaking with the entire poetic tradition in which *Aletheia* represents the essential value and unequivocally announcing his desire to secularize poetry," Simonides replaces "an exceptional and privileged mode of understanding with the most 'political' and the least religious type of knowledge."[21] D&G's valorization of free opinion and their understanding of it as a form of secularized knowledge that has its place in the sphere of the political life of the city are, unmistakably, indebted to Detienne's account. This is also, I would hold, the strongest evidence for the derivation of *doxa* from the earth understood as a sociopolitical milieu of immanence.

As the contention that the philosophers lay claim to an opinion that is different from that of the sophist indicates, there is opinion and opinion. Indeed, opinion is said to take "a truth value" in Greece; hence, "opinion [cannot] be something entirely for the sophists" (147). We thus may have to distinguish between a good and a bad opinion, and D&G's talk of "*free opinion*" therefore gains perhaps a new meaning. It is an opinion that has been freed from bad opinion, an opinion liberated from within opinion without a relation to transcendent knowledge or a standard of truth.

Let me start with bad, that is, unfreed opinion. To do this I focus on an argument made at the beginning of the "Conclusion," where D&G sketch out what amounts to a genesis of opinion. We cling to "fixed opinions," D&G hold, because we need to have some order in our ideas, and, to secure such an order for our ideas, we postulate that there is an equal order among things or states of affairs in the shape of a presumed "objective antichaos" (201–2). Indeed, by recognizing certain qualities of things and perceiving them in conformity with the past, we arrive at fixed opinions. This point has already been made extensively in the chapter "Prospects and Concepts," where, basing themselves on an essay by Hegel, "Who Thinks Abstractly?," D&G argue that "opinion is an abstract thought" in that an opinion "extracts an abstract quality from perception and a general power from affection" (145).[22] This process of extraction of abstract qualities is intrinsically linked to the process of recognition. D&G aver: "Opinion is a thought that is closely molded on the form of recognition—recognition of a quality in perception (contemplation), recognition of a group in affection (reflection), and recognition of a rival in the possibility of other groups and other qualities (communication). It gives to the recognition of truth an extension and criteria that are naturally those of an 'orthodoxy' " (145–46).[23] An opinion in this sense, D&G hold, is therefore, "already political" (145): "The essence of opinion is will to majority and already speaks in the name of a majority" (146). But it is only the "Conclusion" that explicitly states what already has been implicitly advanced in these remarks about opinion, namely, that we "*make an opinion* for ourselves, like a sort of 'umbrella,' which protects us from chaos" (202). In fact, opinion (and thus also a certain politics) serves as a defensive shield against chaos.

As we have already seen, philosophy is involved in a struggle against chaos, and so are the arts and the sciences. But, in distinction from opinion's defense against chaos, "art, science, and philosophy require more: they cast planes over chaos" (ibid.). Rather than protecting themselves against chaos, art, science, and philosophy "tear open the firmament" (ibid.; see also 203–4) religiously woven by opinion and populated by dynasties of gods. Rather than shielding themselves from it, they dive head-on into chaos. They "plunge into the chaos" (ibid.), selecting within it the diagrammatical elements that will constitute the plane of immanence that they drive through it before populating it with their respective ideas. As shown by the talk about plunging into chaos, not only the risks that come with exposing oneself to its abyss but also the notion that the philosopher, the artist, and the scientist "bring back [something] from the chaos" (ibid.), "the *struggle against chaos* does not take place without an affinity with the enemy" (203). Although contending with chaos, the three disciplines of thought also have a constitutive attraction to it. In the case of philosophy, it is a question of "how to retain infinite speeds while gaining consistency," whereas the sciences relinquish chaos's infinite speed (118), and the arts, in a way, restitute it, or, rather, conserve it in all its disturbing force. By selecting within the infinite movements of chaos the elements to construe an Earth, Nature, and a Cosmos, respectively, the struggle in question of the three forms of thought is one by which not only the philosopher but also the artist and the scientist resist death by risking death, as Deleuze had already suggested in "What is a Creative Act?" All three "have resistance in common—their resistance to death, to servitude, to the intolerable, to shame, and to the present" (110). But the "affinity with the enemy" in the struggle that the three forms of thought wage against chaos has still another reason. Indeed, chaos, against which "people are constantly putting up an umbrella that shelters them" (203), is enlisted by philosophy, the arts, and the sciences in the war they wage against opinion understood as that from which comes the "the misfortune of people" (206). D&G sum this up when they write: "It is as if the *struggle against chaos* does not take place without an affinity with the enemy, because another struggle develops and takes on more importance—the struggle *against opinion,* which claims to protect us from chaos itself" (203). And, with respect to art: "A work of chaos is certainly no better than a work of opinion; art is no more made of chaos than it is of opinion. But if art battles against chaos it is to borrow weapons from it that it turns against opinion, the better to defeat it with tried and tested arms" (204). Opinion as that from which the misfortune of people devolves is thus the critical target of all three forms of thought, including philosophy.

In *What Is Philosophy?,* D&G's objections to opinion even go as far as to reject all attempts, in particular those by phenomenology, to rehabilitate opinion as a constituting foundation of all cognition and action in the lifeworld in the shape of "original opinions which bind us to the world as to our homeland (earth)" (149). Husserl's and Merleau-Ponty's conception of an *Urdoxa* distinct from *doxa*—which for these philosophers is not less problematic than for D&G, yet not because they oppose *doxa* to truth or episteme but because they hold it to be a mode of representation corrupted by the understanding of Being and objectivity particular to the modern sciences—is the object of repeated criticism by our authors. D&G's misgivings against the proto-beliefs of an *Urdoxa* consist, basically, in the assertion that, in the same way as opinions, an original opinion is of the order of a proposition (142), that is, a type of prospect. An opinion is "*a function or a proposition whose arguments are perceptions and affections*" (144). They are generated through the extraction by a subject, who identifies himself with a generic agent holding communal beliefs, of some quality from a given perceptive-affective lived situation, a quality that in the form of a statement or proposition lays claim to being commonly accepted (145). The original opinions of *Urdoxa* are not different. They too are of the order of propositions and, hence, not concepts, which alone are capable of becoming the foundation of a homeland, or earth. As D&G note, "the *Urdoxa* does not raise us to the level of the concept" (149). Indeed, "[a] concept is not a set of associated ideas like an opinion. Neither is it an order of reasons, a series of ordered reasons that could rigorously constitute a kind of *Urdoxa*" (207). A concept, in turn, becomes an opinion once it is made into a proposition: "*in becoming propositional, the concept loses all the characteristics it possessed as philosophical concept:* its self-reference, its endoconsistency and its exoconsistency" (137–38). The criticism of *doxa* and *Urdoxa* thus, is conducted in the name of the concept, that is, at the same time, in the name of philosophy.

And yet, in "Example 11" D&G reassert that opinion in the shape of free opinion is one of the fundamental traits of philosophy as a Greek thing. In the context of a critical evaluation of the phenomenology of art developed by Erwin Strauss, Maurice Merleau-Ponty, and Henri Maldiney, they write: "The Greeks with their cities, and phenomenology with our Western societies, are certainly right to consider opinion as one of the conditions of philosophy. But, by invoking art as the means of deepening opinion and of discovering original opinions, will philosophy find the path that leads to the concept? Or should we, along with art, overturn opinion, raising it to the infinite movement that replaces it with, precisely, the concept?" (150). Given the vehement criticism they lead against opinion, it looks, at first, as if D&G's sole aim is to deny any philosophical role to this notion. The phenomenologists' attempts to found philosophy using art to deepen opinion by a regress to an *Urdoxa* are futile. Rather, the path to philosophy as concept creation seems to require the use of art to overthrow opinion. But, as also becomes manifest from this passage, philosophy must replace opinion by "raising it to the infinite movement"—that is, in the shape of free opinion—for the passage to the concept to become possible. If the concept must overturn opinion to be a philosophical concept, the opinion that it replaces must in turn have been the opinion liberated in the sociopolitical and immanent milieu of Greece, and not any vulgar or ordinary form of opinion that still yields to a standard.

As we have seen, concepts cannot be translated into propositions without becoming "more-or-less plausible opinions without scientific value" (79). This statement is followed by the passage in which D&G introduce the third feature of philosophy as something Greek, which I need recall here once again: "But in this way we encounter a difficulty that the Greeks had already come up against. This is the third characteristic by which philosophy is thought of as something Greek: the Greek city puts forward the friend or rival as social relation, and it lays out a plane of immanence—but it also makes *free opinion* (*doxa*) prevail" (ibid.). It now becomes clear that these three characteristics concern only the sociopolitical milieu that the city offers and in which philosophy develops; more precisely, they are the de facto conditions for the emergence of philosophical thought. As a social space that furthers equality, citizens have the right, the freedom, to express their opinions. It is in this milieu that philosophy flourishes, but the free proliferation of opinion imposes on it a specific task that is itself also intrinsically Greek and that also seems to respond to the question left in abeyance about the usefulness of philosophy. Having said that the Greek city "also makes *free opinion* (*doxa*) prevail," D&G go on to say that "philosophy must therefore extract from opinions a "knowledge" that transforms them but that is also distinct from science. The philosophical problem thus consists in finding, in each case, the instance that is able to gauge a truth value of opposable opinions, either by selecting some as more wise than others or by fixing their respective share of the truth" (ibid.). I am tempted to interpret these lines as suggesting two different tasks of philosophy: on the one hand, the task of raising opinion in the sense of free opinion to the level of the concept, thus extracting a "knowledge" from free opinion that is distinct from that of the sciences (thereupon inaugurating philosophy as concept creation), and, on the other, making philosophy useful (and in the same breath legitimizing it) by trying to glean among competing opinions the truth value that allows it to settle their clash once and for all. Indeed, by falling back on dialectics ("interminable discussion") and "universals of contemplation" (Plato), "universals of communication" (Aristotle), "universals of reflection" (Kant), or "speculative proposition[s]" (Hegel) to freeze the opposite and rival opinions and to establish a standard to measure their value, philosophy, in Nietzsche's diagnosis that D&G emphasize, has also compromised itself and shown "bad taste . . . : a reduction of the concept to propositions like simple opinions" (79–80). Bad taste in philosophy consists, above all, in arguing for its usefulness. If the model of knowledge that guides the philosophical task of seeking to settle by way of mediation, for example, the clash of opinions in the marketplace is that of a truth standard, it is not distinct from scientific knowledge. Yet, as at best a "higher opinion," it is a scientific knowledge without any value: "The dialectic claims to discover a specifically philosophical discursiveness, but it can only do this by linking opinions together. It has indeed gone beyond opinion toward knowledge, but opinion breaks through and continues to break through. Even with the resources of an *Urdoxa,* philosophy remains a doxography" (80). In the face of the reign of free opinions, a certain philosophy thus seems to be stuck in an aporia, not only to have to condemn opinion in the name of knowledge, or to seek to extract truth from opinion—a true opinion (see "Example 11")—which, however, would be propositional in nature, that is, nonphilosophical, but also to have to resort to opinion, discursivity, and propositions to express something that in essence is of the order of the concept.

Indeed, at this juncture D&G begin to speak of the paradoxical nature of philosophy. After their claim that philosophy with all its resources remains a doxography, they remark that if philosophy, this Greek thing, is "paradoxical by nature, this is not because it sides with the least plausible opinion or because it maintains contradictory opinions but rather because it uses sentences of a standard language to express something that does not belong to the order of opinion or even of the proposition" (ibid.). Indeed, if philosophy "develops in paradox" (82), it is because, at the same time that it is doxographical, it is para-doxical as well, that is, as Roland Barthes has pointed out, against *doxa,* aiming at something radically beyond *doxa,* which is to say also beyond a concept of truth distilled from opinions. In fact, as D&G hold, the concept is not about truth at all. The relation of thought with the true is much too ambiguous, they hold, for it to be invoked to define philosophy (54). "Philosophy does not consist in knowing and is not inspired by truth. Rather, it is categories like Interesting, Remarkable, or Important that determine success or failure" (82), that is, categories that, as Nietzsche held in "Philosophy During the Tragic Age of the Greeks," are testimony to the particular form of taste required by philosophical thought.[24] The third characteristic of philosophy as something Greek is not simply that it promotes free opinion (as a de facto condition for its emergence) but also that it incessantly struggles with opinion. Even though philosophy from Plato on, that is, beginning with the search for universals to mediate the conflict between rival opinions, sought to overcome opinion by way of truth, philosophy is Greek not only because it is essentially atheist (nonreligious, nontheological) and nonreferential (that is, not scientific) but also because it is fundamentally para-doxical, in a radical break with the opinion that it presupposes, although it can accomplish this only in a relentless struggle with opinion. D&G conclude: "Philosophy thus lives in a permanent crisis" (ibid.). Originating in response to the emancipation of opinion from all subjugation to a standard of truth in the Greek sociopolitical milieu of immanence, philosophy radicalizes such opinion in the shape of the created concepts and thus, in a way, engenders a knowledge that is no longer tributary to opinion. Plato, and most philosophers after him, discarded opinion altogether; for D&G, by contrast, the free opinion that characterizes the sociopolitical milieu of the Greek city is a blueprint for the concept, as it were. And yet, they too cannot but also think of philosophy as an attempt to overturn opinion, however free it may be, to replace it with what they term "concept." While presupposing opinion as free opinion, philosophy cannot but also continue to contest the opinion, however free, that emerges in the Greek democratic milieu, thus putting philosophy into permanent crisis. This, then, is the third characteristic of philosophy as something Greek: "The plane takes effect through shocks, concepts proceed in bursts, and personae by spasms" (ibid.).

But a question remains in abeyance. If free opinion is, indeed, a condition of philosophy, this condition is, first of all, a de facto condition that corresponds to the *isegorical* nature of the city (the right to free speech and to have an opinion). But the conditions in question also have a transcendental sense, as is manifest from the intrinsic nature not only of the friend as a conceptual persona within philosophy but also of the plane of immanence on which concepts are created, and, hence, free opinion as well must be in some way a de jure condition. What, then, is it within philosophy that corresponds to the liberation of opinion in the civic space? Can it be thought without reducing it either to the concept in the traditional sense or to *doxa*? Or does the intuition of the plane of immanence and the creation of concepts on it accomplish a liberation of thought that is only more radical than the one brought about by the emancipation of opinions in the public space? In analogy to what is the case with free opinion in the Greek public space, would such liberation of thought consist in a liberation from all usefulness? The answer to these questions, which is not to be explicitly found in *What Is Philosophy?*, may be that "*free opinion*" as one of philosophy's internal conditions is what D&G in passing refer to as "pure opinion." But what can pure opinion be but an opinion that has been liberated from its opposites, truth, theoretical knowledge, or episteme? In short, "free opinion" as one of the three, specifically Greek features of philosophy may have to be understood as an opinion that is autonomous and whose meaning is not delimited by an outside, such as its traditional opposites, but that is created by itself and that opens up an element within philosophical thought that allows for the creation of concepts to have a place where they can take place to begin with.

In conclusion to this chapter I return to the issue of the nature of the concept, that is, of its reality, raised in the "Introduction." Philosophers have not been sufficiently concerned with it, D&G assert. They have preferred to conceive of the concept "as a given knowledge or representation," that is, formed by way of abstraction or generalization by certain faculties. "But the concept is not given," D&G rebut; "it is created; it is to be created. It is not formed but posits itself in itself—it is a self-positing. Creation and self-positing mutually imply each other because what is truly created, from the living being to the work of art, thereby enjoys a self-positing of itself, or an autopoetic characteristic by which it is recognized. The concept posits itself to the same extent that it is created. What depends on a free creative activity is also that which, independently and necessarily, posits itself in itself: the most subjective will be the most objective" (11). As a creation—and here an additional implication of "creation" comes into view—the concept is like a living being or a work of art, autonomous, which means a self-positing entity. It is not a given (neither native nor innate) autonomy (that faculties can form or employ), but one that posits itself in itself. In a way what is truly created is at the same time self-created. This autopoetic autonomy of the concept as a created entity is "philosophical reality" itself. As we will see hereafter, this distinction between givenness and self-positing autonomy is of further importance to gauge the full impact of the argument that philosophy as the creation of concepts is a Greek thing. This question of autonomy will perhaps also help us further clarify how the third characteristic of philosophy as a Greek thing—that is, its response to "free opinion"—is linked to the earth as autochthonous in a new way.

7

The Fractalization of Greece

At the beginning of this book, I grappled with the statement that "an Autochthon [is] a power of the earth that follows [*suit,* or *suivre,* being an important verb for D&G] a maritime component that goes under the sea to reestablish the territory (the Erechtheum, temple of Athena and Poseidon)" (86). This statement is made in the context of contrasting the kind of deterritorialization that occurs from above in the city-states as imperial states, as a result of which the territory has become desert earth to be reterritorialized by a celestial Stranger, namely, Apollo, to the kind of deterritorialization that takes place through immanence in the city-state as a city. I wish to make a further, and final, attempt to unpack and decrypt this difficult passage, whose difficulty derives, as we will see, not only from the translation of the original into English but to some degree also from a difficulty of translation within the French original itself. What I seek to understand is how the Autochthon—autochthonous Athens, or its autochthonous citizens—who has been liberated through a deterritorializing immanence, composes as a power of the earth with a maritime component that goes under the sea to reestablish, or to reterritorialize, the territory in the shape of the Erechtheum, that is, the temple of Athena and Poseidon on the Acropolis. Obviously, the talk of a maritime component that goes undersea makes little sense. To further clarify the passage in question, I base myself once again on Sissa's and Detienne's *The Daily Life of the Greek Gods,* which, as the context proves, has been one of D&G's acknowledged sources.

I recall that from the beginning a violent power struggle, at times a head-on clash, opposed Athena and Poseidon with respect to the Attican territory: "Each produced evidence of their power in the territory. Poseidon struck a rock with his trident, and the sea water gushed forth right there in the middle of the Acropolis: irrefutable proof that the Lord of the Sea reigned over the highest part of the city . . . Athena, for her part, made an olive tree grow from the disputed land."[1] When the dispute is finally settled by a court in which all men voted for Poseidon and the women, who were more numerous and thus victorious, favored Athena, the resentful Poseidon not only made sure that, henceforth, women were deprived of the voting right that up to then they had enjoyed; he also "made the sea rush in, right up to the Eleusis."[2] This struggle between the powers of the earth and the sea in the constitution of autochthonous Athens is further evidenced on the occasion of the first war that the city had to win. This is the war between Athens under its king Erechtheus, born from the earth, and Eleusis, the territorial base of Poseidon, whose inhabitants had treacherously enlisted foreigners, the savage Thracians, to destroy the autochthonous city. Erechtheus dies mysteriously in the battle. Some texts suggest that he is killed by Poseidon, whose trident plunged "into the Acropolis . . . opened up a tomb for Erechtheus, who was swallowed up by the earth."[3] Walter Burkert in *Homo Necans* describes the mark of Poseidon's trident as "that little bit of 'sea' in the Erechtheum," the depression made being "filled with salt water."[4] Rammed into the earth by Poseidon's trident, Erechtheus, a power of the earth, thus goes undersea, as it were. Anyway, Athena "put a stop to the violence of the god of the seas and pinned Poseidon down with his victim," ordering the construction of the Erechtheum as a sanctuary of both Erechtheus, "the Most Chthonic One, whose body, enclosed in the Acropolis rock, helped to strengthen the foundations of both the city and its very autochthony," *and* Poseidon, the god of the maritime element, who thus is "now integrated into authochthony."[5] Indeed, the Erechtheum, which housed the statue of Athena Poliades as well as a single altar dedicated to both Poseidon and Erechtheus, is the temple of Athena and Poseidon, as D&G note, since Erechtheus (according to Euripides's lost tragedy *Erechtheus*) took the name of his murderer.[6] Indeed, in Athens Erechtheus and Poseidon are in fact merely two names for one single god, *Poseidon Erechtheus,* as Walter Burkert has argued on the basis of the fragment that remains of Euripides's tragedy.[7]

At this point, it becomes inevitable to look once again at the passage that we are seeking to illuminate: "an Autochthon [is] a power of the earth that follows a maritime component that goes under the sea to reestablish the territory (the Erechtheum, temple of Athena and Poseidon)." All the evidence we have provided so far does not seem to fully clarify it, or rather comes to an abrupt stop before the assertion that "a maritime component . . . goes under the sea." Although the passage does not immediately become clearer when we go back to the French original—"*une puissance de la terre qui suit une composante maritime, qui passe elle-même sous les eaux pour refonder le territoire*"—after translating the French into French, it soon becomes evident that the referent of the second "qui" is not "une composante maritime" but, on the contrary, "une puissance de la terre." Retranslated into English, the sentence then speaks of "a power of the earth that follows a maritime component, [the former of] which goes under the sea." In sum, then, as a power of the earth, the Autochthon follows a maritime component, and it is this power of the earth itself (rather than the maritime component) that, in D&G's words, goes under the sea to reestablish (*refonder*), or reterritorialize, the territory.[8] In retrospect, all the mythological lore on which I have relied to dispel the enigmatic character of the passage leads me to recognize the decisive importance of the maritime element for a conception of an autochthony that is no longer earthbound.

To extrapolate the implications of autochthony as a power of the earth that not only has a maritime component but also gives this component an unprecedented leverage in the constitution of autochthony, I turn now to the paragraph that immediately follows the passage on Erechtheus and Poseidon that I have commented upon, which speaks of the "fractal structure" of Greece and the peninsula's relation to the sea. But what is a fractal? The noun and adjective were coined by Benoit Mandelbrot, drawing on the Latin adjective *fractus* and the verb *frangere,* to break, in order to designate discontinuous shapes, such as a coastline. The question of the essence of a coastline like that of Britain set off his research, which is indented by "bays and peninsulas revealing ever-smaller subbays and subpeninsulas—at least down to atomic scales." Mandelbrot's concern consisted in finding a way to measure such non-Euclidean fractal lines, and he discovered that such measurements were a function of the scale of measurement, with the paradoxical result that, ultimately, such lines are infinitely long; in short, they crowd "infinite length . . . into a finite area."[9] Of course, D&G borrow the term from Mandelbrot, although what interests them is not the measurement of such irregular lines but their discontinuity; more precisely, their indentation, the deep recesses that are set into such lines through which, in the case of a coastline, the sea presses inside the land. Of Greece D&G assert that "each point of the peninsula is close to the sea" (87). Indeed, in addition to its mountainous landscape, a major feature of the Greek landscape is that "the sea is always less than 100 km away from any point of the territory where one happens to find oneself, and, conversely, when one sails in the Aegean Sea, one never has to travel more than 60 km in order to reach land that always remains in sight."[10] Rather than being isolated and closed upon itself (self-sufficient and autochthonous in a narrow sense), each point of Greece opens upon the open sea, through which it becomes deterritorialized. Each point also has, therefore, an irregular shape; it is not a well-rounded whole but divided from within by the shores of Greece that "have great length" and through which it is inexorably exposed to the other that comes across the waters.[11] Each point, that is, each city, of Greece has, as D&G say, a fractal structure; in other words, it has an irregular and fragmented shape in the sense that, through its porousness and the rate of flow by which it is exposed to the outside, it exceeds in dissymmetric fashion its topological dimension. Each point of the topological space of Greece is pulled inside out, as it were, by its openness to the sea, that is, to the fluid medium, in which encounters with the other, the stranger, can occur.

A first implication of this fractal nature of Greece is that each city, particularly autochthonous Athens, is a commercial city. Even though the Greek cities are not the first commercial cities, what is singular about them is that, although close to the Orient, they are still separate enough from it to be able to install a new model for social relations and what later will be called "a new imperialism." I quote:

> They are the first to be at once near enough to and far enough away from the archaic eastern empires to be able to benefit from them without following their model. Rather than establish themselves in the pores of the empires, they are steeped [*elles baignent,* they are immersed] in a new component; they develop a particular mode of deterritorialization that proceeds by immanence; they form a *milieu of immanence*. It is like an "international market" organized along the borders of the Orient. (87)

Rather than following the Oriental model of imperial verticality, the polis is a horizontal milieu free of all hierarchical structures for its citizens. But that milieu knows no enclosures: it exceeds the spatial dimensions that would constitute it as an interiority. As we have seen, the Erechtheum, at the center of autochthonous Athens, is the temple both of the fabulous king Erechtheus, son of the Earth, reared by Athena, and of Poseidon, the god of earthquakes, of water, and also, though only secondarily, of the sea. The sanctuary that dominates the center of the city houses both the first born of the Earth and the one who, as his title suggests, makes the earth tremble and extends the milieu of the polis outward upon the sea. As we have seen so far, the Greek polis is the result of a thorough deterritorialization of the earth that effectuates a sociopolitical milieu of immanence in which its inhabitants can freely compete with one another. With its openness to the sea, the city-state also leads to a reterritorialization upon the sea with the result that navigation becomes one of its principal vehicles of exchange, making it the colonizing and commercial power in the Mediterranean.

The polis itself is thus like a fluid expanse in which all its free and mobile citizens compose a whole insofar as they are first in commercial relations with others. The artisans and merchants who are steeped in this milieu of immanence find here, as D&G remark, "a freedom and mobility denied to them by the empires. These types come from the borderlands of the Greek world, strangers in flight, breaking with empire and colonized by peoples of Apollo—not only artisans and merchants but philosophers" as well (87). The milieu of immanence offered by the polis is not just any milieu. It is not a middle as a space of mediation and of reconciled opposites, a space of speculative fullness. As a milieu of artisans, merchants, and philosophers, the polis exceeds all mediating closure upon itself. It is defined by the attraction that it exerts upon artisans and merchants, as well as upon the philosophers who come to it from abroad as a place to think in competition with other thinkers. As Clémence Ramnoux, but also Nietzsche, has pointed out, the philosophers were to a large extent foreigners, and pre-Socratic philosophy, significantly enough, emerged toward the end of the seventh and beginning of the sixth century B.C.E. along the borders of the Orient in Ionia, that is, in Asia Minor, before it wins over the extreme West, Sicily and Italy. It is also in the sixth century that the first schools of philosophy emerged, which also happened to admit among human beings those "others" that are women such as the Pythagorean philosopher Theano or, though much later, slaves such as Epictetus who taught Stoicism at Nicopolis and Rome.[12] Following Ramnoux, D&G write: "Philosophers are strangers, but philosophy is Greek" (ibid.). The word "philosopher," no doubt, was invented by Heraclitus, but the correlate word, "philosophy," is Platonic, in short, Greek.[13] Anyway, the Greek polis, with its fractal nature and openness to others, is not only characterized by its commercial relations; it is also a haven for philosophers. Indeed, it is in Greece that these foreigners, lovers of a kind of wisdom that already takes them out of the company of the sages, find an opportunity to do something that (rather than being something foreign) is essentially Greek—philosophy. It is worth noting here not only that philosophy as essentially Greek develops in Greece thanks to the attraction that its milieu offers to strangers but also that the stranger as a question and a topic is an intrinsic part of its discourse and concern at least from Plato on. In the context of a discussion of the figure of the Stranger (*xenos*) in Plato's *Sophist,* a note in the chapter "Conceptual Personae" that refers to Jean-François Mattéi's *L'Etranger et le simulacre: Essai sur la fondation de l'ontologie platonicienne* (222n6) shows that, in thinking about philosophy as a Greek thing, D&G take into account not only the fact that it is a stranger from Elea who in Western philosophical thought makes for the first time the point that dialogue, even though far from being a peaceful and amiable exchange, is founded by logos in reason but also the fact that the speculation about the relation between self and other, that is, the dialectic of identity, is also an unmistakably Greek problematic.[14] Furthermore, by contending that nonbeing is and that in some regards being is not, this Stranger in the dialogue critically takes on within Greek thought Greek thought itself, or more precisely, the fundamental foundation of the Greek way of conceiving of identity, and within this thought engages in nothing less than a kind parricide of the father figure Parmenides. Indeed, in this late dialogue of Plato, the genre itself of the other (*heteron*) as opposed to the same irrupts into Greek thought. Thanks to the philosophy of the Stranger, "a new way of saying and thinking the same" thus takes place, and "categories that until then remained excentric" now gain access into the heart of philosophy, language, and being itself.[15] As is also evident from the *Statesman,* the stranger is an active persona in Greek philosophical thought, and so is the topos of the stranger and the other itself. Since the Greeks, this concern with the other has remained a hallmark of philosophical thought in the West.

D&G ask: "What do these emigres find in the Greek milieu?" D&G answer:

> At least three things are found that are the de facto conditions of philosophy: a pure sociability as milieu of immanence, the "intrinsic nature of association," which is opposed to imperial sovereignty and implies no prior interest because, on the contrary, competing interests presuppose it; a certain pleasure in forming associations, which constitutes friendship, but also a pleasure in breaking up the association, which constitutes rivalry . . . and a taste for opinion inconceivable in an empire, a taste for the exchange of views, for conversation. We constantly rediscover these three Greek features: immanence, friendship, and opinion. (87–88)

D&G refer here to conditions of philosophy that are unmistakably historical, sociological, and psychosocial in nature and that developed in Greece, especially at its borders with the Orient but also at any of the points within the peninsula because of their proximity to the sea. These are the de facto conditions that made it possible (but as we have seen not necessary) for philosophy to develop. These factual conditions attracted the landless strangers from the Orient—the soon-to-be philosophers—to a land divided from within by its coastline, a land without interiority, which is thus geographically speaking at the edge. They themselves also became part of these de facto conditions under which alone the development of philosophy became a possibility. But such a milieu of immanence, a type of social relation such as friendship, and a taste for opinion are conditions that not only attract foreigners but also, at the same time, make of all the participants in this milieu foreigners in a certain way. If the philosophers become Greek insofar as what they are doing in Greece is philosophy, the Greek autochthon becomes, as D&G

remark (in the context of a discussion of the deterritorialization and reterritorialization involved in the becoming of philosophy), a "stranger to himself, his class, his nation, and his language . . . Becoming a stranger to oneself, to one's language and nation, is not this the peculiarity of the philosopher and philosophy, their 'style,' or what is called a philosophical gobbledygook?" (110; trans. mod.). It is the case, therefore, that what the philosophers develop under the de facto conditions in question is something that is itself specifically Greek, namely philosophy as a kind of thinking that is not territorially rooted but universal, or, as we have seen, concerns the earth itself. As I have already pointed out, the milieu of immanence that characterizes the Greek polis is not a milieu in the sense of a speculative middle of reconciled opposites. This is further evidenced by the fact that the de facto conditions for thinking that the émigrés from the Orient discover in Greece are not conditions of "a softer world." Even though the new kind of autochthony that prevails in the democratic city is no longer one that is brought about through violent and bloody sacrifices, pure "sociability [also] has its cruelties, friendship has its rivalries, and opinion has its antagonisms and bloody reversals" (88).

It is precisely this observation that friendship also has a cruel side that sparks D&G's first explicit reference in *What Is Philosophy?* to the "Greek miracle," which I discussed at some length at the beginning of this book. D&G write:

> Salamis is the Greek miracle where Greece escapes from the Persian empire and where the autochthonous people who lost its territory prevails on the sea, is reterritorialized on the sea. The Delian League is like the fractalization of Greece. For a fairly short period the deepest bond existed between the democratic city, colonization, and a new imperialism that no longer saw the sea as a limit of its territory or an obstacle to its endeavor but as a wider bath of immanence. (Ibid.)

Unlike the eternal beauty free of all local, or national, traces that constitutes the Greek miracle for Renan, it is the battle of Salamis that is the paradigm of the miracle in question for D&G, because it shows in the most precise way what Greek autochthony implied. The autochthony that is freed in the milieu of immanence characteristic of the polis presupposes a deterritorialization, that is, a detachment from the native land, and ultimately, in the case of the Greeks, a reterritorialization on the maritime element. By falling back onto the sea during the Persian War and retrenching on their fleet, that is, onto the "wooden wall" in Herodotus's words, the Greeks became *aporoi,* to use a term that he employs in *The Histories* to describe a nomadic people, that is, the Scyths, who thus defeated the Macedonian army, a term that Liddell and Scott translate as "*impossible* to have any dealing with."[16] By reterritorializing themselves onto the sea after the Persians advanced on Athens and the Acropolis was burned, the Greeks made themselves "unmanageable," impossible to oppose or conquer, and they, in effect, defeated Xerxes's fleet. For D&G, this reterritorialization of the Greek onto the maritime element has a philosophical implication. Through it, they became radically autonomous, autochthonous, but in a new sense. This autochthony gained by the ability to fall back onto the sea after having lost the land and to make themselves *aporoi,* this is, in truth, the Greek miracle according to D&G. It thus not only consists in having been able to create an autochthony of their own by neutralizing the powers of Gaia through a political procedure that deterritorializes the Earth, which, subsequently, is reterritorialized upon the agora and the marketplace, as well as the high sea; by moving from the firm land onto the maritime element, becoming nomadic and *aporoi,* the Greek miracle also consists in founding a plane of immanence that both accommodates the stranger and allows the Greeks themselves to relate to one another as foreigners, who are landless, uprooted, and nomadic—an immanent plane without transcendence.

8

Earth-Thought

Admittedly, the Greek miracle lasted only "for a fairly short period," but, to quote Renan again, even though, in accordance with the nature of a miracle, it also happened only once, its effect may last forever. Now, let me recall that everything that D&G have said so far about the Greek miracle concerns exclusively the factual, that is, sociohistorical, conditions of philosophy in Greece. As I have already intimated, notwithstanding the fact that "philosophy's link with Greece . . . seems a recognized fact" (88), there is no straight and necessary connection between the de facto conditions and philosophy's actual emergence in Greece as an autonomous form of thought. Undoubtedly, as we have seen, certain conditions, especially the political constitution of the polis, favored the emergence of philosophy. Thus Vernant writes that "in its form, philosophy is directly linked to the spiritual realm that we have seen give order to the city, and which was so distinctly characterized by the secularization and rationalization of social life."[1] Referring to pre-Socratic philosophy, he further points out that "there was a profound structural analogy between the institutional space in which the human *cosmos* was expressed itself and the physical space in which the Milesians projected the natural *cosmos*."[2] The link between the two—that is, on the one hand, the sociopolitical milieu with its equalities and symmetrical structure and, on the other, the plane of immanence of philosophy—is, as D&G write, "marked by detours and contingency" (88). At this juncture of their argument in *What Is Philosophy?*, I return to a distinction that has already been broached but whose crucial importance only now comes clearly into view. This distinction is between relative and absolute deterritorialization. By inquiring into it, we will be led back to the three fundamental traits of *autochthony*, *philia*, and *doxa*, yet this time as the transcendental, or de jure, conditions of philosophy as something Greek.[3]

In the chapter "Conceptual Personae," D&G wonder whether there are "not also territories and deterritorializations that are not only physical and mental but spiritual—not only relative but absolute in a sense yet to be determined" (68). This question concerns not only the difference between the friend as a psychosocial type in the Greek milieu of immanence and the friend as a conceptual persona intrinsic to philosophy but also the conceptual personae themselves whose role it is,

D&G aver, "*to show thought's territories, its absolute deterritorializations and reterritorializations*" (69). Indeed, everything that we have seen so far about the Greek miracle—its physical, social, and psychological conditions—is based on a relative deterritorialization. The latter is the condition for the absolute deterritorialization of philosophy itself, one that is spiritual, rather than physical and mental, and that, as the word "absolute" suggests, is severed from the physical, social, and psychological stratum over which it hovers like the metaphysical fumes of the Stoic incorporeals that survey, or skim over, the real at infinite speed. In addition, D&G submit that the vapor of the incorporeals, or concepts, in no way resembles the bodies from which they rise with the effect that "there remains only an allusion" in them to their bodily substrate and that, consequently, philosophy itself (in a sentence missing in the translation) can be said to be "like a gigantic allusion" (159; trans. mod.). In a first approximation one would be tempted to understand the relation between relative and absolute deterritorialization along the Marxist infra- and suprastructure divide, that is, the divide between the material and economic stratum of a society and the ideological, or doxical, stratum on top of it that serves to cover over the former's true nature. But, as D&G note, "even if the word *absolute* turns out to be exact, we must not think that deterritorializations and reterritorializations of thought transcend psychosocial ones, any more than they are reducible to them, or to an abstraction or ideological expression of them. Rather, there is a conjunction, a system of referrals [*renvois*] or perpetual relays" (69–70). D&G describe in some detail how to conceive of this system that is not of the order of a reflection but of referrals and relays, in particular in relation to the sociopsychological type of the friend and the conceptual persona of the friend. They argue that the features of the conceptual personae entertain "relationships with the epoch or historical milieu in which they appear that only psychosocial types enable us to assess," but they also hold that, "conversely, the physical and mental movements of psychosocial types" in a specific historical milieu "become susceptible to a determination purely of thinking and of thought that wrests them from both the historical state of affairs of a society and the lived experience of individuals, in order to turn them into the features of conceptual personae, or *thought-events* on the plane laid out by thought or under the concepts it creates. Conceptual personae and psychosocial types refer [*renvoient*] to each other and combine without ever merging" (70). Later in the chapter of "Geophilosophy," D&G again make the point that "the connection of ancient philosophy with the Greek city and the connection of modern philosophy with capitalism are not ideological and do not stop at pushing historical and social determinations to infinity so as to extract spiritual figures from them," this time, however, to argue for an intrinsically critical, if not utopian, relation between philosophy and the specific period in which it emerges (99). Before I continue with this issue, however, I must elaborate a bit more on the distinction between relative and absolute deterritorialization and reterritorialization.

D&G state:

> Whether physical, psychological, or social, deterritorialization is relative insofar as it concerns the historical relationship of the earth with the territories that take shape and pass away on it, its geological relationship with eras and catastrophes, its astronomical relationship with the cosmos and the stellar system of which it is a part. But deterritorialization is absolute when the earth passes into the pure plane of immanence of a Being-thought, of a Nature-thought of infinite diagrammatic movements. Thinking consists in stretching out a plane of immanence that absorbs the earth (or rather, "adsorbs" it). (88)

The passage warrants a detailed commentary. First, it is essential to note that relative deterritorialization concerns the earth as a planet in three respects: its relationship to the geographical territories that through its history have been carved out on it, to what Carl Schmitt has called the "*nomos* of the earth."[4] Relative deterritorization also includes the earth's relationship to its physical, chemical, and biological history, as well as its relationship to the physical universe and the cosmos in the sense of the stellar system. If D&G have any pressing ecological concerns with the earth as a physical environment and body within the stellar cosmos, it is thus only from the perspective of relative deterritorialization, which itself is only the condition, although in no deterministic sense, of an altogether different concern with the Earth as the Earth of philosophy and of the philosopher. In absolute deterritorialization an Earth emerges that is an exclusive entity of thought, an autonomous Earth that is thought, a thought Earth, or Earth-Thought, for which relative deterritorializations provided certain conditions that favored its emergence but in no way made it unavoidable. As the case of the autochthon demonstrates, relative deterritorializations achieve only a freedom from territories of the earth, a self-positing that, subsequently, can reterritorialize itself on another such territory, like the sea. By contrast, in absolute deterritorialization the earth as a whole is deterritorialized to become Earth-Thought, and as such it is one side of the plane of immanence, namely, Being, or Nature, or the Sensible, the other side being Thought itself. When the earth passes into the pure plane of immanence of thought, when it is absorbed, or ad-sorbed, by thought according to its three modes—philosophical, scientific, or aesthetic thought—the earth becomes Earth, Nature, or Cosmos respectively.

In all three cases we are thus dealing with an earth entirely different from the one that is the object of relative deterritorialization. The difference between both earths comes into view even more forcefully when it is pointed out that absolute deterritorialization not only "does not preclude reterritorialization but posits it as a creation of a future new earth" (88), rather than just a new territory. Now, in particular, in the context of reterritorializations that follow upon absolute deterritorialization, creation is not only linked to that of a future new earth and "a people to come," but also such creation is interlinked above all with philosophical thought, less explicitly with the arts, and is not mentioned with respect to the sciences. Let us remind ourselves again of the creative nature of philosophy, the sciences, and the arts. Creation, D&G tell us, "is to resist" (110) the earth in its present condition, bringing thus an additional aspect of creation to light. They write: "We lack creation. *We lack resistance to the present.* The creation of concepts in itself calls for a future form, for a new earth and people that do not yet exist. . . . Art and philosophy converge at this point: the constitution of an earth and a people that are lacking as the correlate of creation" (108). This motif of utopia that emerges with the subsequent reterritorialization of absolute deterritorialization is, as is evidenced by the chapter on "Geophilosophy," indicative of a certain proximity of D&G to the Frankfurt School, particularly to Theodor W. Adorno's negative dialectics (99). D&G continue: "Actually, *utopia is what links* philosophy with its own epoch, with European capitalism, but also already with the Greek city. In each case it is with utopia that philosophy becomes political and takes the criticism of its own time to its highest point. Utopia does not split off from infinite movement: etymologically it stands for absolute deterritorialization but always at the critical point at which it is connected with the present relative milieu, and especially with the forces stifled by this milieu" (99–100). But D&G also admit that, given the meaning this word has in public opinion, "perhaps utopia is not the best word" to designate the absolute deterritorialization that philosophy performs in relation to relative deterritorializations in the sphere of the present, making the latter "pass over the plane of immanence as movement of the infinite and suppress[ing] it as internal limit, *turn[ing] it back against itself so as to summon forth a new earth, a new people*" (99–100).

In following up on how absolute deterritorializations are to be thought in relation to relative deterritorializations whose fields are, as we have seen, not only historical and psychosocial but also geographical and cosmic, we will perhaps gain insight into the kind of relation that links the de facto conditions of philosophy to the emergence of philosophical thought as something specifically Greek. But to further explain how "absolute deterritorialization takes over from a relative deterritorialization in a given field," an additional distinction, in fact, "a major difference," is introduced, namely, "whether relative deterritorialization takes place through immanence or through transcendence. When it is transcendent, vertical, celestial, and brought about by the imperial unity, the transcendent element must always give way or submit to a sort of rotation in order to be inscribed on the always-immanent plane of Nature-thought. . . . Thinking here implies a projection of the transcendent on the plane of immanence" (88–89). When a deterritorialization devolves from an imperial unity or a spiritual empire such as that of monotheism (or from both, as in political theological conceptions), its projections upon the plane of immanence create and populate it with figures that in paradigmatic fashion refer to the transcendent entities in question, through which a correspondence, a resemblance, between the two orders is achieved. Among the examples given are "Chinese hexagrams, Hindu mandalas, Jewish sephiroth, Islamic 'imaginals,' and Christian icons" (89). In all these cases, the projection of the infinite transcendent entity onto the plane of immanence "is a wisdom or a religion—it does not much matter which" (ibid.). In passing, D&G remark that the sciences and the arts also think through figures that are referential, but rather than laying claim "to prohibited resemblance . . . they emancipate a particular level so as to make it into new planes of thought on which . . . the nature of the references and projections change" (89–90).

From all the preceding developments it is clear that not only philosophy, art, and the sciences but also religious thought presuppose a plane of immanence. Yet, since religion in all its forms plants figures onto the plane that it, like the three forms of thought, requires as well—figures that are in essence projections of something transcendent onto its surface—D&G feel compelled at this juncture to revise their initial claim "that the Greeks invented an absolute plane of immanence" (90). Indeed, the Figures that religion creates on the plane, which entertain a relation of resemblance with the transcendent of which they are the flattened projections, compromise the absolute immanence of the plane. But why, precisely, is such a revision required? Undoubtedly, the qualification "absolute" concerns immanence rather than the plane. As things look now, the specific originality of the Greeks consists not in having invented from scratch a plane of absolute immanence but, with the invention of the concept, in having come up with something that precludes all transcendence and that is thus the source for the absolute immanence of the plane on which they are created. If, indeed, "immanence can be said to be the burning issue [*la pierre de touche brûlante*] of all philosophy" (45), the question becomes one concerning what it is that makes the plane of immanence absolutely immanent. The answer to this question is that only the concepts make the plane's immanence absolute. Indeed, D&G now hold that:

> the originality of the Greeks should rather be sought in the relation between the relative and the absolute. When relative deterritorialization is itself horizontal, or immanent, it combines with [*elle se conjugue* (italics in the original)] the absolute deterritorialization of the plane of immanence that carries the movements of relative deterritorialization to infinity, pushes them to the absolute, by transforming them (the milieu, the friend, and opinion). Immanence is redoubled. This is where one thinks no longer with figures but with concepts (90)

—that is, philosophically rather than in religious, or even scientific, fashion. The Greek originality lies in joining together the relative deterritorialization of the horizontal "milieu of immanence," constituted by "pure sociability," the society of friends, and "the taste for opinion," and the absolute deterritorialization of the plane of immanence performed by thought. Their originality consists in pushing the accomplishments in the realm of the social to the absolute in thought, raising them to a maximum of power in creating an ideal sphere that horizontally doubles and "repeats" the equally horizontal plane of societal immanence. This repetitive doubling that takes place exclusively within the plane of immanence—it is immanent to the plane of immanence, if one may say so—undercuts all verticality and, hence, all referential relation between the immanent milieu, pure sociability, and opinion, and the concepts of milieu, friend, and opinion are "only" absolutizations or infinitizations of the movements characteristic of the political, social, and psychosocial level.[5] I forego D&G's further elaborations on the nature of the concept (as opposed to the figure) and retain only their claim that "concepts are flat surfaces without levels, orderings without hierarchy" (90). But what should retain our attention as well is the fact that, while recognizing "disturbing affinities" between figure and concept "on what seems to be a common plane of immanence" (91), they tend to hold the concepts created on the plane of the "completely different immanence of the absolute" (92), that is, of philosophy, to be fundamentally distinct from the figural projections of the transcendent in, say, Chinese thought. They write that, at best, "all that can be said is that figures tend toward concepts to the point of drawing infinitely near to them" (ibid.). As demonstrated by their discussion of whether something like "Christian philosophy" exists, the threshold between concept and figure is "the atheism of the concept" (92).[6]

The same holds for "Chinese, Hindu, Jewish, or Islamic 'philosophy'" (93). One can speak of such types of thought as "philosophies"

> to the extent that thinking takes place on a plane of immanence that can be populated by figures as much as concepts. However, this plane of immanence is not exactly philosophical, but prephilosophical. It is affected by what populates and reacts on it, in such a way that it becomes philosophical only through the effect of the concept. Although the plane is presupposed by philosophy, it is nonetheless instituted by it and it unfolds in a philosophical relationship with the nonphilosophical. (Ibid.)

Christian, Chinese, Hindu, Jewish, and Islamic thought, to name only these, take place on a plane of immanence, but that does not, therefore, render it philosophical. The criteria for thought to be philosophical in a strict sense concern how this common, still nonphilosophical plane is populated and how it is transformed by what is created on it. Only concepts, not figures, can turn the nonphilosophical plane of immanence into an absolute plane, the plane on which, and within which, philosophical concept-creation can take place. With this we return again to the question of the "Greek miracle." The fact that the plane of immanence shared by all forms of thought can be populated by figures rather than by concepts, as seems to be the case of all the 'philosophies' referred to, shows that concept creation and the concomitant transformation of the nonphilosophical plane of immanence into a philosophical one are nothing obvious at all. In the end, the reference to all the so-called 'philosophies' suggests "that a creation of concepts or a philosophical formation was not the inevitable destination of the plane of immanence itself but that it could unfold in wisdoms and religions according to a bifurcation that wards off [*conjurait d'avance*] philosophy in advance from the point of view of its very possibility" (ibid.). In other words, rather than philosophies, the 'philosophies' in question are not only forms of wisdom, or religions; they are also forms of thought that from the beginning seek to stave off concept creation and, hence, the development of philosophy. Playing on the resources of the expression "*conjurer d'avance*" used here by D&G, one could go as far as to say that these forms of thought are 'philosophies' only to the extent that their thinking by way of figures is a form of plotting, or conspiring, to make the advent of philosophy, and with it, of course, a conception of autonomy and a practice of freedom, impossible from the start. The Greek miracle is a miracle, first of all, for having resisted this general and dominant temptation. In addition, it is a miracle because, as we have already seen, no necessity caused it to happen in Greece. As D&G note, "what we deny is that there is any internal necessity to philosophy, whether in itself or in the Greeks (and the idea of a Greek miracle would only be another aspect of this pseudonecessity). Nevertheless, philosophy was something Greek—although brought by immigrants" (ibid.). Nothing within philosophy itself requires its actualization. It is not a possibility in an Aristotelian sense but perhaps what Deleuze terms a virtuality. It is nothing inevitable. Nor is there any internal reason why philosophy had to emerge in Greece, and, consequently, the miracle that after all happened in Greece is even greater. But, as suggested by the parenthetical statement that the idea of a Greek miracle is only another aspect of a pseudonecessity, to speak of what happened in Greece in terms of a miracle takes the very miraculousness out of the miracle since the idea of a "miracle" is still a function of a necessity, however fictitious it may be. Furthermore, the miracle, or, rather, the event of philosophy in Greece, is all the greater in that philosophy as something specifically Greek was brought to Greece by foreigners, who were given the opportunity in the Greek milieu to develop this form of thought. This, then, is also the point where D&G provide an additional argument to explain what caused the contingent emergence of philosophy in Greece. They write:

> The birth of philosophy required an encounter between the Greek milieu and the plane of immanence of thought. It required the conjunction of two very different movements of deterritorialization, the relative and the absolute, the first already at work in immanence. Absolute deterritorialization of the plane of thought had to be aligned or directly connected with the relative deterritorialization of Greek society. The encounter between friend and thought was needed. In short, philosophy does have a principle [*raison*], but it is a synthetic and contingent principle—an encounter, a conjunction. (Ibid.)

It is, of course, the notion of encounter that should interest us here in explaining the Greek miracle, the miracle of the birth of philosophy in a specific geographical location called "Greece." For philosophy to emerge, the Greek milieu (that is, everything that the Greeks accomplished through relative deterritorialization) not only had to be exposed to the plane of immanence of thought; the Greeks also had to be exposed to it as something foreign, as something that came from the outside through emigrants from the Orient. Conversely, one could also argue that philosophical thought emerges within Greece itself through the encounter of the other, or stranger, which the Greek milieu of immanence made possible for the first time and who from then on became a major conceptual persona in philosophy itself. An encounter is one only if it is with a foreigner, or stranger, making what emerges from the encounter forever open to the other. As we know from *Difference and Repetition,* an encounter is a violent happening between dissimilar things—here, between relative and absolute deterritorialization, more specifically between the social and political democratic frame of Greek society and the thinkers from abroad (even though, as Nietzsche says somewhere, they were not all too popular), more generally between the specific reality of Greek society and thought itself. An encounter is a synthesis, that is, according to Kant's definition of synthesis, a conjunction of two ontologically distinct things, as in the case of a statement that asserts something about an object that is not analytically contained in its concept. Philosophy thus has no intrinsic necessity. On the contrary, to bring it about required the contingency of an inevitably violent encounter and synthetic conjunction, a "heterogenesis." It also could not have happened or could have happened differently.

In "Example 7" one reads that "it is pointless to seek, like Hegel and Heidegger, an analytic and necessary principle that would link philosophy to Greece" (94). As is suggested in *What Is Philosophy?,* Heidegger's reflections on Being and beings bring "Earth and territory together" and, thus, get close to the thought of deterritorialization.[7] However, by arguing that "the specificity of the Greek is to dwell in Being," and by limiting the reterritorialization of the deterritorialized earth onto the "Greek's own language and . . . linguistic treasure—the verb to be," Heidegger, at the same time, "betrays the movement of deterritorialization because he fixes it once and for all between being and beings, between the Greek territory and the Western Earth that the Greeks would have called Being" (94–95). But what precisely is the objection here? As D&G underline, in distinction from Hegel, Heidegger "views the Greek as the Autochthon rather than as the free citizen" (94), that is, as one who continues to be linked to the earth, which at best is deterritorialized so as to signify only "the Western Earth . . . called Being." But am I correct to suspect that it is above all Heidegger's reterritorialization of the earth on the Greeks' own (proper) language and its linguistic treasury that D&G find problematic, because it is limited and excludes exposure to otherness? Is it Heidegger's concern with what is proper that restricts his understanding of the autochthon whose self-positing implies for D&G, as we have seen, an essential openness to the other? Or, differently worded, do D&G believe that Heidegger's emphasis on the proper, on what is truly one's own, continues to be an infatuation with the native and the land and that this obsession blocks the infinite movement of deterritorialization characteristic of philosophy? I leave these questions standing. By contrast, what Hegel and Heidegger still have in common is that they have "conceived of the relationship of Greece and philosophy as an origin and thus as the point of departure of a history internal to the West, such that *philosophy necessarily becomes indistinguishable from its own history*" (95). Yet, as we have already seen, philosophy as a Greek thing is not an origin: first, because nothing necessarily brings it about in Greece, and it, thus, just as well could have happened elsewhere; second, because it is not comparable to a seed from which something grows and develops as a necessary unfolding of possibilities that lay in waiting. "Hegel and Heidegger," D&G write, "remain historicists inasmuch as they posit history as a form of interiority in which the concept necessarily develops or unveils its destiny" (ibid.). But, as D&G contend, if this is so, then it is difficult to understand "the unforeseeable creation of concepts" that characterizes philosophical thought as such (ibid.). Indeed, even though philosophy appears in Greece, that which thus comes into being, when correctly understood in terms of absolute deterritorialization and the creation of concepts, is characterized by a principle that prevents it from being an origin. In *What Is Philosophy?* one reads: "The principle of reason such as it appears in philosophy is a principle of contingent reason and is put like this: there is no good reason but contingent reason; there is no universal history except of contingency" (93).

At this juncture in the chapter "Geophilosophy," D&G return to the question of geophilosophy to expressly disconnect philosophy and the creation of concepts from history. In their words: "Philosophy is a geo-philosophy [hyphenated in the original] in precisely the same way that history is a geo-history [hyphenated] from Braudel's point of view. Why philosophy in Greece at that moment? . . . Geography is not confined to providing historical form with a substance and variable places. It is not merely physical and human but mental, like the landscape. Geography wrests history from the cult of necessity in order to stress the irreducibility of contingency" (95–96). Geophilosophy is not modeled after the form/matter divide. It is not to suggest, especially, that the earth provides the places (according to a certain order, such as from East to West) and respective times (such as the rising and setting of the sun) for philosophy and the concept to arise and unfold according to a history that is internal to them. And finally, rather than establishing the necessity of philosophy's emergence, to speak of geophilosophy is to emphasize the contingency of philosophy's appearance. To say "geo-philosophy" is to say that the only good reason for philosophy to have emerged in Greece is contingent reason and that such contingency is essential to philosophy.

Being intrinsically connected to deterritorialization, that is, to a concern with the earth and, as we have seen, with another or new earth, philosophy is an activity that arises without any intrinsic or necessary relation to a particular site in, precisely, such a site. Indeed, if philosophy is the creation of concepts, and if, as has been shown, such creation presupposes an affirmative belief in this world, then philosophy cannot be riveted to a particular geographical place. For philosophy to be involved in the earth, as the deterritorialized par excellence, it must be without any permanent roots in any native ground. Geophilosophy, paradoxically, implies that philosophy is autochthonous, self-made, a self-positing construct. Furthermore, it is this contingent relation to the geographical space in which it makes an unforeseen act of presence that both prevents it from being an origin and at the same time renders its contingent repetition possible in other places on the earth. Its geo-philosophical nature allows it, in D&G's terms, *to become,* rather than to evolve historically, that is, in a linear or circular manner (95). Some of these points are further stressed in the following.

In consent with Braudel's studies, the additional observation is made that, besides wresting "history from the cult of necessity in order to stress the irreducibility of contingency," geography also "wrests it from the cult of origins in order to affirm the power of a 'milieu' (what philosophy finds in the Greeks, said Nietzsche, is not an origin but a milieu, an ambiance, an ambient atmosphere: the philosopher ceases to be a comet)" (96). The reference is one to "Philosophy During the Tragic Age of the Greeks" and shows that what D&G have called "milieu" so far broadly corresponds to what Nietzsche had simply called "culture," or, more precisely, "a real Culture, fashioned in a homogeneous style." I think that, in view of what D&G understand by philosophy, it is also important to point out that for Nietzsche the culture that provided the context for the birth of philosophy, rather than reflecting a time of decline, was one in which the Greeks found themselves "in good fortune, in mature manhood, [in] the midst of the fervent serenity of a brave and victorious man's estate [*der feurigen Heiterkeit des tapferen und siegreichen Mannesalter*]."[8] In such a milieu, the philosopher is no longer an unpredictable and terrifying figure in the sky but an integral part of the milieu in its own right (*gerechtfertigt*), that is, fully immanent within this milieu, or culture, even though this does not necessarily mean that he enjoys popular applause.[9] According to Nietzsche, the Greeks alone accomplished this, doing so at the climax of their agonal culture. Geography, D&G continue, wrests history "from structures in order to trace the lines of flight that pass through the Greek world across the Mediterranean" (96). Geography detaches history from the stifling complex of beliefs and the constrictive arrangement of the institutions of a society to which it is tied, opening it to lines of flight that, rather than fleeing life, "produce the real, . . . create life," by opening it up to the other, to relations to the other that do not originate in a location but that pass through it, traced by the other, as it were.[10]

D&G go on:

> Finally, [geography] wrests history from itself in order to discover becomings that do not belong to history even if they fall back into it: the history of philosophy in Greece must not hide the fact that in every case the Greeks had to become philosophers in the first place, just as philosophers had to become Greek. "Becoming" does not belong to history. History today still designates only the set of conditions, however recent they may be, from which one turns away in order to become, that is to say, in order to create something new. The Greeks did it, but no turning away [*détournement*] is valid once and for all. (96)

"Becoming" is a crucial, technical term of Deleuze's thought, and would certainly require a lengthy development. Let it suffice here if I retrace this concept back to Nietzsche's statement that "becoming must be explained without recourse to final intentions; becoming must appear justified at every moment . . . The present must absolutely not be justified by reference to a future, nor the past by reference to the present."[11] By contrast, I wish to linger here for a moment on the connection made by D&G between the notions of "becoming" and "turning away [*détournement*]." In "Example 7," the term had already been mentioned in connection with Heidegger's understanding of the accomplishment of the Greeks. There D&G write that:

> In Heidegger it is not a question of going farther than the Greeks; it is enough to resume their movement in an initiating, recommencing repetition. This is because Being, by virtue of its structure, continually turns away when it turns toward, and the history of Being or of the Earth is the history of its turning away, of its deterritorialization in the technico-worldwide development of Western civilization started by the Greeks and reterritorialized on National Socialism. (95)[12]

"Turning away" thus translates Heidegger's notion of the withdrawal of Being in all of Being's turns (or epochs) and amounts to a movement of the deterritorialization of Being, or the Earth. Deterritorialization as a movement of turning away, as a *Kehre* away from Being, or the Earth, an *Abkehr* from the Earth, is thus required for something new to happen, for something to become. By highlighting nonhistorical becomings, in advance of the history that will absorb them as moments in a teleologically oriented process, geography thus also permits understanding philosophy in terms of the movements by which it turns away from its history to reinvent itself again from scratch, in advance of this history, that is, in terms of philosophy's event-character (96). To the question "why philosophy in Greece at that moment?," geography stresses the singularity of what happened there, or, rather, of what became there, namely that "at that moment" when the Greeks became philosophers, the philosophers became Greek. Without the happening of this becoming, which is not yet an event, there would be no history of philosophy in the first place. Geography thus also names the moments at which a turn away from the earth happens for a becoming to become possible, one that, at the same time, is reterritorialized onto Greece. I repeat: At the same moment when the Greeks became philosophers, the philosophers became Greek! Is this not what Deleuze, in *Difference and Repetition,* had already called "the Greek propitious moment [*l'heureux moment grec*]"?[13]

However, "no turning away is valid once and for all" (96). The Greeks did it, but no turning away from the earth to the Earth keeps forever. Let us remind ourselves again with Renan that the Greek miracle happened only once. From what we have seen so far, it seems as if it is in the nature of philosophy to happen only once, to be a miracle of sorts, contingent, without necessity. It seems as if philosophy forever will have been only something Greek, and, should it already have happened again or, perhaps, happen again in the future, the contingency of its occurrence will cause it to be Greek again. D&G write: "Philosophy appears in Greece as a result of contingency rather than necessity, as a result of an ambiance or milieu rather than an origin, of a becoming rather than a history, of a geography rather than a historiography, of a grace rather than a nature" (96–97). But, if this is so, another question arises: "Why did philosophy survive Greece, or after Greece?" (97; trans. mod.). If, indeed, the emergence of philosophy is a miracle, it could only have happened once, as suggested by Renan. No repetition with a difference of it would seem to be possible. Before I follow D&G through their answer to the question of why philosophy survived after Greece, which implicitly contains another reservation regarding the notion of "miracle," I briefly turn to Frédéric de Towarnicki's interview with Jean Beaufret quoted in *What Is Philosophy?* I do so because what D&G are up against is perhaps more tangible in Beaufret's comments about the uniqueness of philosophy as an exclusively Greek thing. Paraphrasing Heidegger, Beaufret says, "No one has a monopoly in relation to the source. The source is everywhere, undetermined, Chinese, as well as Arab and Indian . . . Heidegger evokes 'a few other great beginnings besides the Greek sending.' But then there is the Greek episode, the Greeks having had the strange privilege to call the source Being, and they did this on the basis of something that is specifically Greek, and unheard of, namely the *difference* between Being and beings."[14] Even though the *Schritt zurück* is possible everywhere, even in languages that do not know the verb "to be," "Being, for its part, is not ecumenical; its name is Greek, and it comes to nobody's mind to force people to be Greek! In all of the history of philosophy, Heidegger has been the only one to have had a sense of this originary limitation of what is in question in philosophy from one end to the other." Because of what is at stake in philosophy with the question of Being, it follows, says Beaufret, that "philosophy is a regional event as it were. The Greeks have never insisted on its universality." By calling the source Being, the emergence of philosophy as the thought of Being in Greece is something restricted to a region, something finite that can lay no claim to universality. Beaufret holds that philosophy "has no pretension of establishing eternal truths. This is one of the great differences between philosophy on the one hand, and, on the other, science and faith. Indeed, there are two forms of the ecumenical, the one of faith and the other of science." By calling the source "Being," philosophy is intimately tied to a language that the Greeks, as Beaufret remarks, "did not interpret as a means of expression or communication. 'Hellinizein . . . to speak Greek, meant, first and foremost, to behave in a Greek manner, in the manner of someone for whom all propositions would be propositions containing the verb being." By understanding philosophy as an essentially Greek thing, one, moreover, that does not lay claim to universals (but is more about a specific manner of existence, the Greek way of being in their milieu) because of its distinction from the arts and especially the sciences, which are concerned with the communication of universals and hence are ecumenical, Beaufret's posthumously published "Libres propos" resonate with several of D&G's statements in their response to their question concerning what philosophy is. But Beaufret's propositions on the regional nature of philosophy (and its lack of pretending to universality) can also serve as a foil against which to determine D&G's response to the question of what made philosophy survive its Greek actualization. Indeed, if philosophy is, as Beaufret pointed out, a "regional event" without any ecumenical ambitions—even though he also admits that "philosophy has long thought that it too is ecumenical"—why was what the Greeks invented 2,500 years ago unheard-of enough "to last and still be of concern to us today"? Beaufret answers that we belong to this origin (*nous sommes de cette nativité*), and philosophy "is the development of a tradition, one source among other sources . . . ."[15] Needless to say, these explanations beg the question, because if philosophy is geophilosophical in the sense that it would be a "regional event," intrinsically finite, and without any ecumenical thrust, then what can it mean to assert that we belong to this origin? We who? Would holding that we belong to the same tradition, furthermore, not also require us to answer the question to what tradition belongs the notion of tradition in question? D&G will spell out a different answer to this question, one that is predicated on the irreducible Greekness of philosophy and that averts assumptions such as "the source is everywhere," nativity, tradition, and so forth, all of which, after all, skirt the uniqueness of the Greek miracle.

If philosophy survived after Greece, philosophy after Greece is, according to D&G, just as little the continuation of the philosophy of Greece as "capitalism during the Middle Ages is the continuation of the Greek city (even the commercial forms are hardly comparable)" (97). Before expanding on the relation of European philosophy to philosophy in ancient Greece, D&G first explore the milieu, that is, the relative deterritorialization that characterizes Europe from the Middle Ages to the present (Braudel is here again their main source), and its relation to the milieu of immanence in ancient Greece. They write: "for always contingent reasons, capitalism leads Europe into a fantastic relative deterritorialization that is due first of all to [*qui renvoie d'abord,* that is, which refers to] city-towns *and that* [capitalism] *itself takes place through immanence*" (ibid.). The deterritorialization of capitalism not only proceeds by way of immanence, that is, in the milieu of the world market, whose centers, however, are in the West, but also is the only one to propagate and to extend even "to the ends of the earth before passing into the galaxy" (ibid.). Even though this relative deterritorialization of capitalism echoes that of the Greek city-states, however, it "is not a result of [*n'est pas la suite,* is not a follow-up on] the Greek endeavor but a resumption [*reprise*], in another form and with other means, on a scale hitherto unknown, which nonetheless relaunches the combination for which the Greeks took the initiative—democratic imperialism, colonizing democracy" (ibid.). For D&G there is no causal relation between Greece and Europe; Europe is not the consequence of or follow-up on Greece. There is no continuity, "*pas de suite,*" between them, and, as a result, no spirit or telos holds sway in the history of the West that would make Greece the origin of European capitalism and philosophy. Certainly, what happens in Europe beginning with the Middle Ages echoes what took place in Greece, but it is an endeavor that takes place through entirely different means and on an entirely different scale. Everything hinges here on the term "*reprise,*" translated as "resumption." Indeed, what happens economically in Europe is also a resumption and a re-launching, "*une reprise*" (a re-covering, re-starting, re-newal, re-petition, and so forth) and "*une relance*" (a term that can also be translated as "revival"), of not merely certain elements but even of "the combination for which the Greeks took the initiative—democratic imperialism, colonizing democracy." With Husserl undoubtedly in mind, but not without some irony, D&G conclude that "the European can, therefore, regard himself, as the Greek [already] did, as not one psychosocial type among others but Man par excellence, and with much more expansive force and missionary zeal than the Greek" (ibid.).

So, if the economic milieu of relative deterritorialization through immanence in medieval and postmedieval Europe is not a continuation of the Greek city-state, how does one have to understand the resumption and relaunching of the specifically Greek combination between colonization and democracy? The answer is provided after a discussion of how philosophy accomplishes absolute deterritorialization in both ancient Greece and European philosophical thought. As D&G note, for Europe to be able to claim the privilege to represent Man par excellence, to claim that in it the "whole of humanity is connected to itself as previously it had been in Greece" (and *not,* as the translators hold, "as it never was in Greece"), thus extending an invitation to all the other parts of the world to Europeanize themselves by reterritorializing themselves onto Europe, it is not enough simply to invoke "the rise 'of philosophy and the mutually inclusive sciences,'" as Husserl did (98). "Rather," D&G contend, "the infinite movement of thought, what Husserl calls Telos, must enter into conjunction with the great relative movement of capital that is continually deterritorialized in order to secure the power of Europe over all other peoples and their reterritorialization on Europe" (ibid.). In other words, for philosophy to be able to claim that it has "universal" appeal, it is not enough for it to merely be philosophy: it must be the result of an absolute deterritorialization that radicalizes on the level of thought the relative deterritorialization accomplished in immanent fashion on the social, political, and economic level of a society. This is what happens in the West, and its philosophy is thus a resumption and relaunching of the originality of Greece, of that for which the Greeks took the initiative. D&G write:

> Modern philosophy's link with capitalism, therefore, is of the same kind as that of ancient philosophy with Greece: *the connection of an absolute plane of immanence with a relative social milieu that also functions through immanence.* From the point of view of philosophy's development, there is no necessary continuity passing from Greece to Europe through the intermediary of Christianity; there is the contingent recommencement of a same contingent process, in different conditions. (Ibid.)

In short, European philosophy is not the continuation or further development of Greek philosophy as an origin. It is "the contingent recommencement of a same contingent process, in different conditions." Thus, European philosophy, in the same way as Greek philosophy, is a unique event, one that stands next to it in its own rights (and limits). But can one speak of something like European philosophy in the same way as one can speak of Greek philosophy? Or is European philosophy, in the wake of Plato, not rather continuing to do what Plato began, namely to compromise the radical nature of what took place with the pre-Socratics by making immanence immanent to something and thus saving the transcendent? In other words, has European philosophy been able to relaunch the Greek enterprise by way of a radical or absolute deterritorialization of the relative deterritorializations accomplished by Western capitalism and thus to create a philosophy that would be its appropriate correlate on the level of thought, the only one that could be said to represent an equivalent to what the Greeks accomplished?

Let me briefly comment on the following remark in "Example 3": "The Greek world that belonged to no one increasingly becomes the property of a Christian consciousness" (46). As demonstrated in the "Example" by the preceding remarks on Kant's discovery of "a modern way of saving transcendence" (ibid.), by making immanence immanent to a pure consciousness, to a thinking subject who is the subject of the field of immanence of all possible experience, the subject as a subjective unity (capable of reflection and self-representation) comes into possession of the field of immanence. By contrast, D&G suggest that the Greek world or Greek (relative) immanence—the societies of friends, democracy, commerce, the reign of opinion—belonged to no one. The same obtains of the radical immanence of early Greek philosophy: it belonged to no one. Once immanence and philosophy becomes a property, an attribute, a belonging of Christian consciousness, it becomes something transcendent to a consciousness or a culture and is no longer immanent. Philosophy is Greek only if it does not belong to anyone, the Greeks included. To say that philosophy is Greek is thus also to say that no Christian, Indian, Islamic philosophy is possible, for this would mean that philosophy belongs or is a property of Christian, Indian, Islamic, Chinese thought and culture. Based on radical immanence, philosophy must be something that cannot be possessed but that can happen or take place in different contexts and worlds. So far, this has been the case only in Greek pre-Platonic philosophy, but not really in what is called European philosophy. Thus far, only one lone philosopher within so-called European philosophy stands out as an exception.

9

Earth, Nature, Cosmos

At this point it becomes inevitable to begin addressing the "history" of philosophy that undergirds *What Is Philosophy?* In doing so we will also have to take up the question of memory with which we opened our investigation of D&G's attempt to reflect back on what it is that they have been doing while doing philosophy. Let us first note that D&G, in a gesture not unlike that of Heidegger, retrace the birth of philosophy in Greece to the pre-Socratics. As opposed to Plato and Aristotle, with whom Greek philosophy reached its unmistakable culmination in the fourth century, and who since then have been heralded as the founders of Western philosophical thought, the much older and, with the rise of Platonism, long forgotten pre-Socratics represent something other for D&G, something more intimately connected to philosophical thought as they understand it. As is clear from "Example 2," Plato, although a master in creating concepts, already betrays the Greek miracle by understanding concepts as representations of a prior objectality, the uncreated or the Idea (29–30). In *Essays Critical and Clinical,* Deleuze even speaks of "the poisoned gift of Platonism" insofar as it introduced transcendence into philosophy.[1] And this betrayal of the plane of absolute immanence that comes into being with the doctrine of the Ideas from there on dominated Western philosophical thought. Again in the same way as Heidegger, who knows only one poet whose poetic saying had the stature of meeting the pre-Socratic's thinking saying, D&G know only one philosopher who has been capable of repeating with a difference what the early Greeks accomplished (and thus to create a philosophy worthy of early European capitalism). Even though on occasion they have some good things to say about Leibniz or Nietzsche, Spinoza is "the prince of philosophers," "perhaps . . . the only philosopher never to have compromised with transcendence and to have hunted it down everywhere" (48). Spinoza, D&G further hold, "is the Christ of philosophers" in that, like Christ, he "was incarnated once, in order to show, that one time, the possibility of the impossible"; he accomplished "the supreme act of philosophy": "he showed, drew up, and thought the 'best' plane of immanence—that is, the purest, the one that does not hand itself over to the transcendent or restore any transcendent, the one that inspires the fewest illusions, bad feelings, and erroneous perceptions" (59–60). Spinoza is the philosopher who "fulfilled [*achevé,* completed] philosophy because he satisfied its prephilosophical presupposition" (48), namely, that All is One, such that "only with the Atheist Spinoza" does philosophy's most proper assumption become fully achieved (92).[2] Spinoza, in short, is the only philosopher in the long history of philosophy who reactualizes in a new and creative way what had been accomplished by the pre-Socratics. He is in no way a continuation of what began at one moment in Greece but reinvents, as if for the first time and in a different fashion, the concern with immanence and the earth. Although a "Spinozist inspiration" happened to Bergson once, specifically, at the beginning of *Matter and Memory* where a plane is marked out that slices through chaos (48–50), nothing much has happened since then. As a consequence, D&G see themselves compelled to ask the question concerning what they have been doing all their lives in doing philosophy with the aim, needless to say, of clarifying whether what they have been doing meets the standards of philosophical thought in the context of modern and contemporary capitalism. "Will we ever be mature enough for a Spinozist inspiration?" (48), they ask in *What Is Philosophy?,* that is, in a work explicitly intended to reflect back on what they have been doing while doing philosophy. While doing philosophy they were too busy and "not sober enough" to ask the question: "There was too much desire to *do* philosophy to wonder what it was, except as a stylistic exercise" (1). But at this late moment in their lives, D&G remind themselves of the fact that philosophy originates in Greece, that, hence, it is a Greek thing by nature, the "Greek miracle" par excellence. And thus, while recollecting what it was that they were doing while doing philosophy, they reconstruct what it is, precisely, that comes into being with the Greeks. But in the chapter "Geophilosophy" they also acknowledge: "We are no longer Greeks" (107). And yet, what they have been doing all their lives has been philosophy, this Greek thing! So, if one can no longer be Greek, then in what sense does one continue to do philosophy, something that by nature is essentially a Greek thing?

Before outlining an answer to this question I wish to follow D&G through another twist of their thought on geophilosophy, more precisely, on how they conceive of modern philosophy, that is, of philosophy as it survives in Europe after its birth in Greece. They submit that modern philosophy, with German Idealism and Romanticism undoubtedly in mind, is characterized by its recollection of its origin in Greece. D&G's own attempt to reflect on what they have been doing in doing philosophy, along with the return to philosophy's origin in Greece to which this reflection invites, is, of course, situated within the contours that define modern philosophy. This relation of modern philosophy to its own past is conceptualized in terms of reterritorialiation. D&G write: "Modern philosophy is reterritorialized on Greece as [a] form of its own past" (101). When speaking of modern philosophy they have German philosophy especially in mind but, first and foremost, Hölderlin—the Hölderlin from the letter to Casimir Böhlendorff whose argument about the ancients and the moderns D&G translate into their own terminology. In this letter, as is well known, modernity is said to live or experience its relationship with Greece

> as the reverse or contrary of the Greeks, the symmetrical inverse: the Greeks kept the plane of immanence that they constructed in enthusiasm and drunkenness, but they had to search for the concepts with which to fill it so as to avoid falling back into the figures of the East. As for us, we possess concepts—after so many centuries of Western thought we think we possess them—but we hardly know where to put them because we lack a genuine plane, misled as we are by Christian transcendence. (Ibid.)

According to D&G, the gist of Hölderlin's argument is the following: "The 'Autochthon' for the Greeks is our 'stranger,' that which we have to acquire, whereas our Autochthon is what, to the contrary, the Greeks had to acquire as their stranger" (ibid.). In a footnote it is pointed out that "even Renan's celebrated text on the Greek 'miracle' has an analogous complex movement: what the Greeks possessed by nature we can rediscover only through reflection, by confronting a fundamental forgetfulness and worldweariness; we are no longer Greeks, we are Bretons" (224n14). In any case, modern and, undoubtedly, contemporary philosophies are the discontinuous and contingent recommencements of the philosophical event that occurred in ancient Greece. Take Hölderlin again: "The Autochthon and the stranger are no longer separate, like two distinct personae, but distributed like one and the same double persona who unfolds into two versions in turn, present and past: what was Autochthonous becomes strange; what was strange becomes Autochthonous. With all his strength Hölderlin calls for a 'society of friends' as the condition of thought, but it is as if this society had suffered a catastrophe that changes the nature of friendship" (102). A new, original conception of the conceptual personae and of the democratic milieu of immanence characterizes modern philosophical thought. Furthermore, by redistributing the same double persona along past and present versions, modern philosophy grounds itself, that is, reterritorializes itself, on ancient Greek thought. Such reterritorialization on its past in Greece seems to be a characteristic feature of what survives of Greek philosophy in the present, suggesting continuity. D&G write: "We reterritorialize ourselves among the Greeks but according to what they did not possess and had not yet become, so that we reterritorialize them on ourselves" (ibid.). But is this double and dialectical reterritorialization by which a continuity between Greece and the present is established not also something specifically new in modern philosophy, something that already sets it thoroughly apart from ancient thought?

Indeed, by recollecting its own past in Greek thought and reterritorializing itself on this past, modern philosophy introduces the notion of continuity into philosophical thought that, at first sight, seems to suggest that modern philosophy follows from Greek thought as a consequence from an origin. However, if Greek thought is not an origin, as we have seen, how are we to conceive of this continuity between the past and what reterritorializes itself upon it? Undoubtedly, such reterritorialization can lead to the erection of the past as an overbearing model for thinking in modernity that stifles all novelty, all creation. But the continuity can also mean doing what the Greeks did, creating concepts on an absolute plane of immanence in an altogether novel, that is, no longer Greek, way. As François Jullien has noted, since Hegel it has been common knowledge that philosophy is a Greek thing, but since Hegel it has also been assumed that philosophy "becomes fully itself only by detaching itself from the idiom in which it first appeared."[3] When D&G ask, "Will we ever be mature enough for a Spinozist inspiration?" (48), the question is also: have we, D&G, ever been mature enough to do today what Spinoza did, namely, to fulfill Greek philosophy beyond its idiom in an absolutely new way by satisfying within, and against, an overwhelming Christian context the presupposition of a radical immanence of the plane of the creation of concepts? Given all the competitors that today lay claim to philosophy, from the human sciences to the media, have we, D&G, when doing philosophy been able to repeat with a difference in today's context what Spinoza and before him the Greeks did, namely drive through chaos a radically immanent plane on which to create new concepts? By inventing new concepts, have they repeated in a discrete way the intuition that drove Greek philosophical thought and re-created it in a new way—in a way that skirts the temptation of claiming to have developed a more universal philosophy by freeing it of its previous idioms though living up to its inspiration? And, in the same breath, have they avoided the temptation of assuming a telos of greater and greater fulfillment of philosophy's project? Have they, indeed, in doing philosophy been able to break with the history of philosophy within that very history, thus becoming, like Greek philosophy, a contingent event of something radically new? The answer to all these questions is *What Is Philosophy?*, with its determination of philosophy as the creation of concepts on a plane of immanence and as one form of thought distinct from the sciences and the arts.

To conclude, let me return again to D&G's acknowledgment that what they have been doing all along has been philosophy. This is a recognition that is also coupled, as we have seen, to the question "What is philosophy?" Their answer in their last book-length study is that philosophy is one form of thought, one out of three, the other two being the sciences and the arts, and that in terms of creativity philosophy holds no privilege over the other two. But the question that has concerned me from the beginning has also been whether philosophy, nonetheless, plays a privileged role in situating the sciences and the arts with respect to itself in this tripartite multiplicity of the forms of thought. I wish to conclude my reading of *What Is Philosophy?*, that is, D&G's answer to this question and hence what they have been doing all along, with a series of further questions concerning the status of philosophy in a work that inquires into the very essence of philosophy but also puts it on equal footing with the sciences and the arts. As I have already pointed out, the distinction between these three forms consists in separating off the sciences (metaphysics) and the arts (the doctrine of beauty) from philosophy in what I described as an unheard-of redistribution in the form of a multiplicity of what historically speaking was intimately interconnected at the beginning of philosophy. Furthermore, the effort of thus parceling out the three forms of thought as a multiplicity pursues the eminently philosophical aim of determining each form in its purity. The concepts that philosophy creates on its plane are irreducible to the functives of the sciences and to the percepts/affects of the arts. Undoubtedly, all three forms of thought interact and give rise to mixtures, interferences, and intersections, but this in no way breaches the purity of each one of them: "The three thoughts intersect and intertwine but without synthesis or identification" (198–99). Each one of the three forms is a creation in its own right, an identity, which in its purity is not affected at all by the existence of the other two. D&G write: "That being so, it is inevitable that philosophy, science, and art are no longer organized as levels of a single projection and are not even differentiated according to a common matrix but are immediately posited or reconstituted in a respective independence, in a division of labor that gives rise to relationships of connection between them" (91). Such relationships occur when, for instance, the sciences transform a concept into a proposition, or philosophy produces the concept of a function, or the arts render sensible a concept or a functive. But, again, this in no way puts the irreducibly distinct purity of each respective form of thought into question.

They are three irreducible forms of thought, which D&G describe as a heterogenesis (199) of thorough identities, in short, of a unity divided within itself by heterogeneous tasks.

Throughout *What Is Philosophy?* the presupposition that the three forms of thought, and their constitutive elements, are absolutely independent identities whose purity can be established without difficulty is never challenged; the fact that philosophy, science, and art intersect and mix only indicates that they remain irreducibly themselves in all these interactions. Only in the concluding paragraph, indeed, only in its last sentence, do D&G acknowledge the possibility of an ultimate undecidability of the three pure forms of thought. At that point they return to the claim that all three disciplines, each one in its own way, are in relation with a negative: philosophy with nonphilosophy, science with nonscience, and art with nonart. Each one of them needs "the No that concerns it" (218) as something that comprehends it. D&G write: "They do not need the No as beginning, or as the end in which they would be called upon to disappear by being realized, but at every moment of their becoming or their development" (ibid.). What comprehends each discipline is the chaos in which they carve themselves out and into which, as three forms of thought, all three plunge in different ways:

> In this submersion it seems that there is extracted from chaos the shadow of the "people to come" in the form that art, but also philosophy and science, summon forth: mass-people, world-people, brain-people, chaos-people—nonthinking thought that lodges in the three, like Klee's nonconceptual concept or Kandinsky's internal silence. It is here that concepts, sensations, and functions become undecidable, at the same time as philosophy, art, and science become indiscernible, as if they shared the same shadow that extends itself across their different nature and constantly accompanies them. (Ibid.)

In short, the nonthinking thought, which in each single form of thought as a form comes into being through the chaos into which each one must plunge to bring back what constitutes it in a specificity properly its own, interlinks and unites all three different forms from within. However, insofar as all three share this relation to chaos and the thinking thought that it entails, they also become ultimately undecidable and indiscernible. In retrospect, it would be necessary to ask whether the consequences of this final insight are at all manifest in what D&G develop with respect to the differences between the three forms of thought. Yet, rather than pursuing this question, let me just wonder from whence this insight into the ultimate undecidability of the identity of the three forms of thought comes. Although the reference to Klee and Kandinsky definitely suggest that art has at least an inkling of the nonthinking thought that from within limits the independence of each form of thought, is it not philosophy again that establishes that this condition affects all three forms, including itself?

There are three forms of thought: philosophy, the sciences, and the arts. Each one is constituted through the institution of a plane of immanence that is either a plane of consistency, of reference, or of composition respectively, which in turn is populated by concepts, functives, or percepts/affects. Concepts are auto-referential, functions referential, and percept/affects concern what has never been felt or perceived before. Whereas the concepts that the philosopher brings back from chaos, or "the land of the dead," are variations, the functions that the scientist brings back from chaos are variables, and the percepts/affects that the artist brings back are sensible varieties never experienced before (202). Within each of the three realms either conceptual personae, partial observers, or esthetic figures accomplish this work. The concepts correspond to events, while the functions concern states of affairs, and the percepts/affects make up monuments (199). In addition, each form of thought has a tripartite structure. I limit myself to the case of philosophy since it is the one in which the point is made most explicitly: "Philosophy presents three elements, each of which fits with the other two but must be considered for itself: *the prephilosophical plane it must lay out (immanence), the persona or personae it must invent and bring to life (insistence), and the philosophical concepts it must create (consistency).* Laying out, inventing, and creating constitute the philosophical trinity—diagrammatic, personalistic, and intensive features" (76–77).

It is certainly the case that time and again D&G suggest that the three forms of thought are a multiplicity of unique forms that, although they are joined together because of the interrelations that exist between them, do not form a unity. At the end of *What Is Philosophy?*, this "*junction*—not the unity—*of the three planes*" (208) is described as a function of the brain, that is, of "the mind itself [*l'esprit même*]" (211). This brain is not the physiological organ that one usually understands by it. D&G submit that it is

> a primary, "true form" as Ruyer defined it: neither a Gestalt nor a perceived form but a *form in itself* that does not refer to any external point of view, any more than the retina or striated area of the cortex refers to another retina or cortical area; it is an absolute consistent form that surveys *itself* [*qui se survole*] independently of any supplementary dimension, which does not appeal therefore to any transcendence, which has

> only a single side whatever the number of its dimensions, which remains copresent to all its determinations without proximity or distance, traverses them at infinite speed, without limit-speed, and which makes of them so many *inseparable variations* on which it confers an equipotentiality without confusion. (210)

In short, the brain that joins all three forms of thought together without unifying them is the "absolute form" (211) of what from the beginning has been defined as the concept. Or, more precisely, it is the concept of the concept. D&G write: "the brain, under its first aspect of absolute form, appears as the faculty of concepts, that is to say, as the faculty of their creation, at the same time that it sets up the plane of immanence on which concepts are placed, move, change order and relations, are renewed, and never cease being created" (ibid.). The brain as that which joins the three disciplines of thought is itself the faculty of concepts, in short the faculty at the root of the discipline of philosophy. The junction that it brings about between itself and the two other forms of thought is said not to be a unity. But is it that simple? Has Deleuze not said himself, in *Proust and Signs,* that multiplicity itself requires some unity? He writes there that "there must be a unity that is the unity of this very multiplicity, a whole that is the whole *of* just these fragments: a One and a Whole that would not be the principle but, on the contrary, 'the effect' of the multiplicity and of its disconnected parts."[4]

The triadic parceling out of the forms of thought—in a movement that, except for the (perhaps) ironic reference to the trinity of philosophy, is never put into question—does several, perhaps three, things with respect to the question of unity. First, the triadic nature of the features that in almost every case suggest three possibilities of multiplicity, and only three—for example, the lexicologically exhaustive distinction between variations, variabilities, and varieties—cannot but suggest that the three forms of thought are all the forms there are, at least in any strict sense.[5] Second, even though D&G argue that there is no matrix from which these three forms could be shown to emerge, that unity and unification are a function of "religious taste" that opinion attributes to the sciences in particular (206), the threesome in question nevertheless suggest completion if not a unitary whole that the three forms exhaust. Third, given that D&G evoke the "philosophical trinity," can one avoid the suspicion that it is philosophy itself that has spearheaded the analysis of the three forms of thought of which it is only one that within the triad in question nevertheless has a special position? Certainly, the sciences and the arts do not need philosophy to reflect upon themselves, as D&G do not tire of telling. And yet, is it not philosophy that assumes a peculiar role in *What Is Philosophy?* in establishing what each form of thought is about? Not only is the first half of the work devoted to answering the question of philosophy, but the titles of the chapters on the sciences, logic, and the arts already clearly indicate philosophy's leading role in that what is specific to them—functives, prospects, percepts, and affects—is established in relation to the philosophical concept. In addition, this dominant role of philosophy in assessing what it itself is and what the other forms of thought correspond to cannot but trigger the question of whether D&G's inquiry into *What Is Philosophy?* is not in essence a self-reflection of philosophy, a "logic of philosophy," say, in the style of Eric Weil, in which categories of philosophy are mustered to reflect on philosophy from within philosophy itself.

In this study I have been primarily interested in figuring out how D&G understand geophilosophy. I have shown geophilosophy to be involved in the Earth as the absolute deterritorialized sociopolitical milieu of immanence that the Greek polis produced through relative deterritorializations. Science, for its part, "takes a bit of chaos in a system of coordinates and forms a referenced chaos that becomes Nature, and from which it extracts an aleatory function and chaoid variables" (206). But what about the arts? In the same way that there are at times in *What Is Philosophy?* terminological inconsistencies with regard to philosophy's and the sciences' respective relationships to the earth and nature, so as regards the arts some ambiguities obtain. Notwithstanding occasional equivocities, it is, nevertheless, safe to state that the arts are involved with the "universe-cosmos" (180), or "planetary Cosmos" (189). The work of art is a monument that, according to D&G, "does not actualize the virtual event but incorporates or embodies it: it gives it a body, a life, a universe." They go on to say that such "universes are neither virtual nor actual; they are possibles, the possible as aesthetic category . . . , the existence of the possible, whereas events are the reality of the virtual, forms of a thought-Nature that survey every possible universe" (177–78). And yet, D&G add: "This is not to say that the concept precedes sensation in principle: even a concept of sensation must be created with its own means, and a sensation exists in its possible universe without the concept necessarily existing in its absolute form" (178). Even though the concept does not de jure precede sensation, nor the Earth the Cosmos, because they are independent entities, the question of the status of the earth with respect to the other two elements of the triad subsists as a question. Yet, does this question subsist merely as one of the transcendental illusions that, as D&G noted at the beginning of their inquiry, are inevitable, illusions that will not fail to come to haunt an approach that seeks to curtail the import of philosophy by giving the sciences and the arts an equal voice in the triad but nonetheless can be brushed off? Or is it not rather a question that is prompted independently of the equal role that the arts and the sciences are said to play in relation to philosophy, by the whole thrust of what D&G have undertaken in *What Is Philosophy?*

A final question! With their respective concerns with the Earth, Nature, and the Cosmos, philosophy, science, and art have parceled out three concerns that in early Greek thought were intimately interlinked. But what about the world? The problematic of the world arises in *What Is Philosophy?* in the context of what D&G call a belief in this world, in an unconditional yes to the world as it is. This affirmation of the world is the philosophical gesture par excellence, which sets it squarely apart from wisdom and religion. Is the world, that is, is this world, then, the overarching unity in which the earth, nature, and the universe-cosmos are distributed, or in view of which philosophy, science, and the arts create? Is "world" the broader philosophical concept in which the Earth as philosophy's proper concern, insofar as it is one form among other forms of thought, is shown to have its place, together with Nature and the Cosmos? Is it not through this concept of world that philosophy, rather than science or art, has surreptitiously guided D&G's inquiry into the three so very different forms of thought that are philosophy, science, and art?

Notes

Introduction

1. François Dosse, *Gilles Deleuze and Félix Guattari: Intersecting Lives,* trans. D. Glassman (New York: Columbia University Press, 2010), 14.

2. Ibid., 456.

3. Ibid.

4. Ibid., 14; Gilles Deleuze, *Negotiations: 1972–1990,* trans. M. Joughin (New York: Columbia University Press, 1995), 155.

5. Dosse, *Gilles Deleuze and Félix Guattari,* 456.

6. Gilles Deleuze and Félix Guattari, *What Is Philosophy?,* trans. H. Tomlinson and G. Burchell (New York: Columbia University Press, 1994), 1.

7. Eric Alliez, *The Signature of the World, or What Is Deleuze and Guattari's Philosophy?,* trans. E. R. Albert and A. Toscano (New York: Continuum, 2004). Alliez absolves himself of this need of retranslation on the basis that D&G's thought is an attempt "to rescue philosophy from the illusion of . . . discursiveness" (23), and the concomitant deluded opinion that concepts can be detached from the philosophical problems to which they are to respond on a plane of immanence. To remain faithful to a philosophy that rejects all transcendence, Alliez's book, with some notable exceptions, endorses D&G's language without any critical distance, and at times even overdoes it in an effort to make their philosophy "revolve around the Spinozist mystery" and "Spinoza's materialist imagination" (ibid).

8. Dosse, *Gilles Deleuze and Félix Guattari,* 15.

9. Deleuze and Guattari, *What Is Philosophy?,* 47.

10. Dosse, *Gilles Deleuze and Félix Guattari,* 456.

Chapter 1

1. Ernest Renan, *Souvenirs d'enfance et de jeunesse* (Paris: Calmann Lévy, 1893), 57–58.

2. Ibid., 59.

3. Ibid., 59–60.

4. Ibid.

5. Jean-Pierre Vernant, *The Origins of Greek Thought* (Ithaca, N.Y.: Cornell University Press, 1982), 103–4.

6. Gilles Deleuze and Félix Guattari, *What Is Philosophy?*, trans. H. Tomlinson and G. Burchell (New York: Columbia University Press, 1994). All page references in the text are to this edition.

7. Gilles Deleuze and Claire Parnet, *Dialogues II*, trans. H. Tomlinson and B. Habberjam (New York: Columbia University Press, 2002), 61. Gottfried Wilhelm Friedrich Hegel, *Philosophy of Right*, trans. T. M. Knox (Oxford: Oxford University Press, 1952), 13. For a refined discussion of Deleuze's relation to Hegel, see Henry Somers-Hall, *Hegel, Deleuze, and the Critique of Representation: Dialectics of Negation and Difference* (Albany: State University of New York Press, 2012).

8. Deleuze, *Negotiations*, 137.

9. Rather than a "stylistic exercise," that is, an obligatory reflection on philosophy in conformity with the rules of the trade, as one is in the process of doing philosophy, the question about the nature of philosophy that D&G pose, at a moment in their lives when they are sober enough to look back upon what they have been doing all along, is of the order of what they term "nonstyle" (1). For an excellent study of the notion of nonstyle in Deleuze, see Donald Cross, "What Is Nonstyle in *What Is Philosophy?*" in *Deleuze and the Schizoanalysis of Literature*, eds. I. Buchanan, A. Tynan, and T. Matts (New York: Bloomsbury Academic, forthcoming 2014).

10. Deleuze, *Negotiations*, 155.

11. Ibid., 154–55 (trans. mod.).

12. Ibid., 147.

13. Gilles Deleuze and Félix Guattari, *A Thousand Plateaus: Capitalism and Schizophrenia*, trans. B. Massumi (Minneapolis: University of Minnesota Press, 1987), 32. See also, Gilles Deleuze, "Théorie des multiplicités chez Bergson," http://www.le-terrier.net/deleuze/20bergson.htm.

14. See also Deleuze and Guattari, *A Thousand Plateaus*, 32–33.

15. Ibid., 73–74.

16. Deleuze and Parnet, *Dialogues II*, ix.

17. Ibid., viii–ix.

18. Ibid., 14.

19. Vernant, *The Origins of Greek Thought*, 130.

20. Marcel Detienne, *The Masters of Truth in Archaic Greece*, trans. J. Lloyd (New York: Zone Books, 1996), 89–106. Regarding the new, centered social space associated with the polis, see also Vernant, *The Origins of Greek Thought*, 125–26.

21. Gilles Deleuze, "Remarques," in *Nos Grecs et leurs modernes*, ed. B. Cassin (Paris: Seuil, 1992), 250.

22. Jean Beaufret, "La naissance de la philosophie," in *Dialogue avec Heidegger: Philosophie grecque* (Paris: Minuit, 1973), 36. He continues: "It is on the shores of Ionia, as well as those of Italy that she was born one day—Mediterranean—before she came, toward the end of the Greek world, to inhabit Attica where she was not so well received."

23. "Libres Propos de Jean Beaufret recueillis par Frédéric de Towarnicki," *Ethernité* 1, no. 1 (Paris: Editions de la Différence, 1985): 92.

24. Beaufret, "La naissance de la philosophie," 19–20. Beaufret adds: "And by the way, the word *philosophia* did not always exist even in the Greek language."

Chapter 2

1. Stephan Günzel, "Nietzsches Geophilosophie und die 'gemässigte Klimazone' im Denken des Abendlandes," *Dialektik* (2000–2001): 17–34.

2. The chapter "Peoples and Fatherlands," from *Beyond Good and Evil,* is, indeed, an examination of the national characteristics not only of philosophy but also, especially, of the arts, with a particular emphasis on music; in short, it is an examination conducted in the spirit of the French moralists who considered themselves unprejudiced and honest observers of national mores. This investigation takes place in light of an eventual unification of Europe, in accordance with what Nietzsche terms "*the soul of Europe*" (182), and for which the French with "their old, manifold, *moralistic* culture," that is, the tradition that spans from Montaigne to Montesquieu, enjoy a definite "superiority over Europe" (193) in contrast to the Englishmen who "are no philosophical race" (189), who, furthermore, firmly cling to Christianity, and the Germans whose atavistic obsession with the soil, "insanity of nationality" (196), and lack of grand style (except the "single species of public and *roughly* artful rhetoric" [184] that reaches them from the pulpit) deprives them of "European *noblesse*" (192). Moreover, what sets France's superiority over Europe apart, especially from Germany, is that, in the same way as England and Italy, it has been able to assimilate the Jews whom Nietzsche characterizes as "the strongest, toughest, and purest race now living in Europe"(187). Indeed, the nomadic race of the Jews offers a definite model for the way Nietzsche conceives of the European soul. This is especially the case when he characterizes the good Europeans as becoming "more and more detached from the conditions under which races originate that are tied to some climate or class; [and becoming] increasingly independent of any *determinate* milieu that would like to inscribe itself for centuries in body and soul with the same demands. Thus an essentially supranational and nomadic type of man is gradually coming up, a type that possesses, physiologically speaking, a maximum of the art and power of adaptation as its typical distinction" (176). Now, it must be noted that what Nietzsche calls nations, peoples, or races cannot simply be identified with geographical regions. Nietzsche's references to the Germans as "the 'people of the middle'" (178), to the north/south divide, and to climate conditions suggest, of course, some sort of topological or geographical framework. But what he offers about the threatening Germanization of all Europe or the Anglicization of France already considerably complicates the fact of assigning peoples to specific geographical locations. What above all makes this difficult is that, according to Nietzsche, "what is called a 'nation' in Europe today . . . is really rather a *res facta* than a *res nata* (and occasionally . . . a *res ficta et picta*) . . . in any case something evolving, young, and easily changed, not yet a race, let alone such an *aere perennius* as the Jewish type" that, for its part, has no particular geographical home (188). In short, it is difficult to see how Nietzsche's characterization of the national characteristics of the French, Germans, and English could lay the foundation of geophilosophy. Let me also add that the only reference to the earth occurs in an aphorism that comes after Nietzsche points out that, apart from mediocrity and a loss of individuality, the democratization

of Europe may result in breeding a new caste of tyrants, including tyrants, that is, geniuses, in the spiritual sphere: "I hear with pleasure that our sun is swiftly moving toward the constellation of *Hercules*—and I hope that man on this earth will in this respect follow the sun's example. And we first of all, we good Europeans!" (177). (Friedrich Nietzsche, *Beyond Good and Evil: Prelude to a Philosophy of the Future,* trans. W. Kaufmann [New York: Vintage Books, 1989].) By contrast, it is in *Thus Spoke Zarathustra* that Nietzsche can be shown to be a philosopher concerned with the earth as distinct from otherworldliness.

3. Fernand Braudel, *La Méditerrané et le monde méditerranéen à l'époque de Philippe II,* 2nd ed. (Paris: Colin, 1960), 295–96.

4. Even though Deleuze's 1987 essay "What Is the Creative Act?" can be read as a template for *What Is Philosophy?* (1991) in many ways, the earth as it figures in this essay, namely as an element, is in no way the earth D&G talk about in this book.

5. Maurice Blanchot, *The Space of Literature,* trans. A. Smock (Lincoln: University of Nebraska Press, 1982), 224.

6. Neither is it the concept of "the planetary ecology as a single living creature, a super-organism," that is, "a global 'organism,'" "replete with feedback loops and stabilizing subsystems," called after the ancient earth goddess. See Jack Cohen and Ian Stewart, *The Collapse of Chaos: Discovering Simplicity in a Complex World* (New York: Viking, 1994), 378, 384, 387.

7. Deleuze and Parnet, *Dialogues II,* 40.

8. Mark Bonta and John Protevi have argued, regarding the term "*terre,*" "there is no consistency in D&G's use of the majuscule in the French text." They may be right, but, just to make sure that I do not miss something, I will regularly correct the uniform translation of the term in *What Is Philosophy?* when, according to the original, "Earth" should be spelled with a capital *E.* (Mark Bonta and John Protevi, *Deleuze and Geophilosophy: A Guide and a Glossary* [Edinburgh: Edinburgh University Press, 2006], 80.) Given that D&G distinguish between the earth as the deterritorialized par excellence and the earth on which the latter is reterritorialized, is it not to be expected that there is a rationale for sometimes spelling "Earth" with a capital *E* and on other occasions with a lowercase one?

9. Deleuze, *Negotiations,* 146.

10. Deleuze and Parnet, *Dialogues II,* 3.

11. Ibid., 18. For an in-depth discussion of the question of metaphor in Deleuze's terminology, see Paul Patton, *Deleuzian Concepts: Philosophy, Colonization, Politics* (Stanford, Calif.: Stanford University Press, 2010), 20–28.

12. As examples of the different uses that D&G make of the terms "deterritorialization" and "reterritorialization," I refer, for example, to their book on Kafka, where the deterritorialization of language and its subsequent spiritual or physical reterritorialization are established as the first characteristic of a minor literature: Gilles Deleuze and Félix Guattari, *Kafka: Toward a Minor Literature,* trans. D. Polan (Minneapolis: University of Minnesota Press, 1986), 18–20. Or take *Anti-Oedipus,* where the terms are used to describe the two directions, or senses, of schizophrenia as a process: Gilles Deleuze and Félix Guattari, *Anti-*

Oedipus. Capitalism and Schizophrenia, trans. R. Hurley, M. Seem, and H. R. Lane (New York: Viking, 1977), 130–31.

13. For a more detailed discussion of all the facets of this notion, see Deleuze and Guattari, *A Thousand Plateaus,* 54–55.

14. Deleuze and Parnet, *Dialogues II,* 36, 40.

15. Ibid., 118.

16. Ibid., 134.

17. Gary Shapiro writes: "Deterritorialization consists in an idealizing movement by which actual physical space becomes subsumed within some structure requiring a more conceptual definition." (Gary Shapiro, "Beyond Peoples and Fatherlands: Nietzsche's Geophilosophy and the Direction of the Earth," *Journal of Nietzsche Studies* 35–36 [2008]: 11.)

18. For the rendering of the French term "*instauration*" by "institution" in the English translation of *What Is Philosophy?,* see Leonard Lawlor, "A Note on the Relation Between Etienne Souriau's *L'instauration philosophique* and Deleuze and Guattari's *What Is Philosophy?,*" in *Deleuze Studies* 5 (November 2011): 400–406.

19. And, conversely, "Perhaps every territory presupposes a prior deterritorialization, or [perhaps] everything happens at the same time": "We cannot even say what comes first" (68).

20. In the original, D&G speak of "*la terre qui redonne des territoires*" (82), which H. Tomlinson and G. Burchell translate as "the earth, which restores territories."

21. But if the earth goes beyond any territory and opens onto an elsewhere, the earth as philosophy's earth is also never fully consummated by a territory such as Greece. As a consequence D&G are made to wonder whether, apart from the territory onto which the deterritorialized earth is reterritorialized, there are not also territories that are "not only physical and mental but spiritual": "What is the Fatherland or Homeland invoked by the thinker, by the philosopher or artist? Philosophy is inseparable from a Homeland [*Natal*] to which the a priori, the innate, or the memory equally attest. But why is this fatherland unknown, lost, or forgotten, turning the thinker into an Exile? What will restore an equivalent of territory, valid as a home? What will be philosophical refrains? What is thought's relationship with the Earth?" (68–69). Later we will encounter the motif of a "new Earth" and the topic of utopia. To be able to answer D&G's question, it would obviously be necessary to explore each one of them in depth.

Chapter 3

1. Renan, "Prière sur l'Acropole," in *Souvenirs d'enfance et de jeunesse,* 69–70.

2. François Lefèvre, *Histoire du monde grec antique* (Paris: Librairie Général Française, 2007), 163; Christian Meier, *The Greek Discovery of Politics,* trans. D. McLintock (Cambridge, Mass.: Harvard University Press, 1990), 73.

3. Nicole Loraux, "Clisthène, diviseur-lieur d'Athènes," in "Territoires, frontières, passages," special issue, *L'inactuel: Psychanalyse & Culture* 8 (1997): 24.

4. Lefèvre, *Histoire du monde grec antique,* 164. By contrast, other scholars,

such as Meier, have pointed out that in spite of its rationality Cleisthenes's reform did not consist in the realization of a theory but was the result of an eminently practical policy. (Meier, *The Greek Discovery of Politics,* 78.)

5. For a detailed account of the complexities of the reform, see Meier, *The Greek Discovery of Politics,* 53–81. Although the reform is the practical realization of *isonomia,* this claim for effective participation in the city did not yet include a claim by the *demos* to government. In fact, at the time, chief functions of the state were still handled by the aristocrats (66–68).

6. Ibid., 79.

7. Ibid., 60.

8. Loraux, "Clisthène, diviseur-lieur d'Athènes," 10.

9. Ibid., 14.

10. Aristotle, "Constitution of Athens," in Aristotle, *Complete Works,* ed. J. Barnes (Princeton: Princeton University Press), 1985, vol. 2, 2354.

11. Ibid., 14. By contrast, in the short reflection devoted to topos and *khora* in *Introduction to Metaphysics,* after having pointed out that the Greeks, rather than understanding the spatial according to extension, experience it "according to place (topos) as *chora,* which means neither place nor space but what is taken up and occupied by what stands there," Heidegger shows topos and *khora* to be intimately interlinked rather than standing in opposition. Topos as *khora,* that is, in the capacity of *khora* is (in the *Timeus,* at least) the "placelike 'space'" into which a thing is set and is set forth from it. *Khora,* in a way, modifies topos. Indeed, for things to be able to have their place, topos needs to be bare of all modes of appearance so that it can be the place in which something becomes, and shines forth from it. This is what *khora* accomplishes with respect to topos. (Martin Heidegger, *Introduction to Metaphysics,* trans. G. Fried and R. Polt [New Haven, Conn.: Yale University Press, 2000], 69–70.)

12. Hesiod, *Theogony,* in *The Homeric Hymns and Homerica,* trans. H. G. Evelyn-White (Cambridge, Mass.: Harvard University Press, 1959), 87 (line 117).

13. Since the last part of this passage above all will need our repeated attention, I cite it in the orginal: "elle libère un Autochthone, c'est-à-dire une puissance de la terre qui suit une composante maritime, qui passe elle-même sous les eaux pour refonder le territoire (L'Erechtheion, temple d'Athéna et de Poséidon)" (83).

14. Immanuel Kant, *Critique of Pure Reason,* trans. P. Guyer and A. W. Wood (Cambridge: Cambridge University Press, 1998), 590.

15. Walter Burkert writes: "The 'sea' and the olive were the pledges the two great gods offered to the city as proof of their power." (Walter Burkert, *Homo Necans: The Anthropology of Ancient Greek Sacrificial Ritual and Myth,* trans. P. Bing [Berkeley: University of California Press, 1983], 157.)

16. See Nicole Loraux, *Born of the Earth: Myth and Politics in Athens,* trans. S. Stewart (Ithaca, N.Y.: Cornell University Press, 2000), 29–30. See also 31.

17. Loraux's work on autochthony has been challenged by Marcel Detienne and Giulia Sissa as one-sided in a crucial chapter to which D&G also refer. Detienne and Sissa forcefully demonstrate that the idea of autochthony is not exclusively a male ideology and praxis. (Marcel Detienne and Giulia Sissa, in *The*

Daily Life of the Greek Gods, trans. J. Lloyd [Stanford, Calif.: Stanford University Press, 2000].)

18. Henry George Liddell and Robert Scott, *A Greek-English Lexicon* (Oxford: Oxford University Press, 1968).

19. Plato, *Republic,* in *Collected Dialogues,* 658–59 (414c–415a).

20. Nicole Loraux, *The Children of Athena: Athenian Ideas About Citizenship and the Division Between the Sexes,* trans. C. Levine (Princeton, N.J.: Princeton University Press, 1993). Of course, Athens was not the only city to claim autochthony. Loraux writes that "each city has a 'first man' as an ancestor, founder, and civilizing or political hero, born of the earth like Erechthonios of Athens, of a river like Phoroneus of Argos, from a marsh such as Alalkomeneus of Boeotia," and so forth (Loraux, *Born of the Earth,* 8). But, as she also shows, the myth of autochthony plays a much more dominating role in Athens than in any of the other cities.

21. Let me point out that, in the *Statesman,* Plato squarely opposes autochthony (*ek ges,* 271a), as a characteristic of the early world age of Kronos, to political life (272a), which characterizes the present age of Zeus. Born from the earth, human beings during Kronos's reign were guarded and presided over by the god, in the same way as human beings today have charge of inferior species of life (271e). Life under Kronos thus did not know any freedom, and there was no political life of its earthborn humans to speak of. As Loraux notes, the Platonic myth of the *Statesman* "is anchored in no space whatsoever, especially not in that of the city" (Loraux, *Les enfants d'Athéna,* 72). Although Plato leaves the question open as to which one of the two ages in question is the happier (272b), the question arises whether D&G, in their attempt to rethink autochthony, underwrite the Platonic assignment of autochthony as being born from the earth to an earlier nonpolitical stage of human life.

22. Indeed, as Loraux's elaborations make clear, even the myth of Erechtheus makes room for sexuality. She writes: "The child is born *both* from the earth and from sexuality" (Loraux, *The Children of Athena,* 58). Thus, without clearly saying it, "the story of [Erechtheus's] birth implicitly provides the model for a declaration of collective autochthony" (69). But both models have something else in common that made it possible for the citizens of the polis to make a simultaneous use of them. Indeed, from what we have seen, both versions demonstrate that Athenian autochthony comes with a price. By opposing triumphant Athenian autochthony to the manifold alterity of the other Greeks, "every sign of deviation [*alterité*] at the heart of the city—beginning with the deviation introduced by women," becomes concealed (220). Since the exclusion of women from the city contains in essence the exclusion of all others, the dogmatic concept of autochthony such as it is represented by the story of Erechtheus shows that this story is invested by "the desire of a society of men to deny the reality of reproduction . . . since masculine experience dictates that what really counts takes place among men" (17). It is invested by the desire to get rid of the other sex, envisioning "the status of the *aner* as lying beyond the opposition between men and women," in short, exclusively from a male perspective (ibid.). Loraux concludes that in both versions "the myth of autochthony is seen as an opera-

tor of exclusion: the original exclusion of 'others.'" As such, the "ideas of autochthony come to contradict and limit that other Athenian representation of Athens, as a city 'open' to foreigners"(246). Indeed, in contrast to the xenophobia that characterized Sparta, the Athenians did not mount crusades in the name of autochthony (Loraux, *Born of the Earth,* 20).

23. In the following I will not distinguish between Erechtheus and Erichthonius (or Erechtheus II), whom some consider to be the son of the former. All the sources I will be consulting to clarify the importance of the figure of Erechtheus for the problematic of autochthony in D&G's *What Is Philosophy?* essentially follow Plutarch and make no distinction between the two. Walter Burkert remarks that "*Erechtheus* and *Erichthonius* are obviously merely variants. Only *Erechtheus* is used in cult, as it is the original, probably non-Greek, name. *Erichthonius,* who is 'peculiarly of the earth,' is a Hellenizing neologism, perhaps taken up in Attic epic because of the etymology. The myth then differentiates between the two by telling of Erichthonius' birth, but Erechtheus' death" (Walter Burkert, *Homo Necans,* 156). As Loraux notes: "With Erichthonios or with Erechtheus (whether or not they are distinguished) begins the long line of Athenian kings" (Loraux, *Born of the Earth,* 31).

24. Loraux, *The Children of Athena,* 51 (emphasis mine).

25. Ibid., 49–50.

26. Ibid., 50.

27. Yet, as Loraux points out, in spite of the Periclean Law from 451–450 that defines the citizen as "one who 'is born from two citizens' . . . in fact there is no such thing as a female citizen, any more than there is a 'female Athenian,'" as a result of which "the Athenian citizen could just as easily be defined as a man who has nothing but citizen-fathers on both sides: his own father, and his mother's father" (Loraux, *The Children of Athena,* 119). Even in its political discourse, the city does not know an autochthonous woman, or an Athenian woman, but only the race of women.

28. Only foreigners would question such inconsistency, Loraux remarks. The Greeks themselves were able to face such contradiction (Loraux, *The Children of Athena,* 57–58).

29. In this version of autochthony, "the dream of an Athens where women are totally excluded" is present, as well (Loraux, *The Children of Athena,* 121).

30. Indeed, I wonder whether Plato's *Menexenus,* in which Socrates recites a funeral oration offered as a model for speaking publicly about the dead that he claims to have been composed by a woman, no less, namely Aspasia, his former teacher of rhetoric, is not at the origin of D&G's reinterpretation of autochthony. This oratory, which parodies official eloquence, is remarkable not only because some of the commonplaces of the *epitaphioi logoi* are ironically pushed to their extreme limit but also because in addressing the issue of the "goodness of [the Athenian citizens'] birth" (237a–b), Socrates starts with a praise of the one mother (237c) from which they all descend as brothers (239a), that is, as equals—the Earth as the motherland, no doubt, but also all the women who have imitated Earth as far as pregnancy and birth is concerned (238a). The political model of autochthony, which is the prime subject of this oratory, is thus

reconceived to the extent that the parental couple is reevaluated in line with the Periclean Law according to which to be Athenian means to have been born from both an Athenian mother and father. As Loraux notes, the implicit critique that one finds in the *Menexenus* of the extreme patrilineal ideology of the actual myths of autochthony is, undoubtedly, an isolated and polemical case in Greece (Loraux, *The Children of Athena,* 121). But it is a philosophico-political critique, and the question, therefore, is whether D&G's interpretation of the theme of autochthony is not at least to some extent indebted to it, rather than to a historical, social, and mythical account of "the goodness of birth."

31. Herodotus still recalls the time when the grand families of Athens boasted of having had a prestigious foreign origin (see Loraux, *Born of the Earth,* 22). One may also wish to point out here that, inasmuch as cult is concerned, the continuity between pre-Greek times and the properly Greek period is, as Walter Burkert has argued, rather astounding (Walter Burkert, *Homo Necans,* 194).

32. Sissa and Detienne, *The Daily Life of the Greek Gods,* 215.

33. Ibid., 218.

34. Marcel Detienne, "Qu'est-ce qu'un site?," in *Tracés de Fondation,* ed. M. Detienne (Louvain-Paris: Peeters, 1990), 4.

35. Sissa and Detienne, 141–42.

36. Detienne, "Qu'est-ce qu'un site?," 2.

37. Marcel Detienne, "Apollon Archégète. Un modèle politique de la territorialisation," *Tracés de Fondation,* 301–11.

38. Ibid., 301.

39. Ibid., 302.

40. Detienne, "Qu'est-ce qu'un site?," 13.

41. Henry George Liddell and Robert Scott, *A Greek-English Lexicon* (Oxford: Clarendon Press, 1978), 252.

42. Pierre Grimal, *The Dictionary of Classical Mythology,* trans. A. R. Maxwell-Hyslop (Oxford: Basil Blackwell, 1986), 47. For my elaboration on the figure of Apollo, I am indebted to this work.

43. Grimal, *The Dictionary of Classical Mythology,* 47.

44. Ibid., 49–50.

45. Detienne, "Apollon Archégète," 303–4.

46. Ibid., 309–10. Detienne's discussion of Apollo's exile from Olympus is in all likelihood a reference to Apollo and Poseidon's revolt against Zeus, as a consequence of which they were banished by Zeus from the heavens and ordered to build the walls of Troy.

47. Detienne, "Qu'est-ce qu'un site?," 13.

Chapter 4

1. Plato, *Collected Dialogues,* 448 (412b).

2. Jean-Pierre Vernant, *The Origins of Greek Thought,* 107–25.

3. Marcel Detienne, *The Masters of Truth in Archaic Greece,* trans. J. Lloyd (New York: Zone Books, 1996), 133.

4. Ibid., 133.

5. Alexandre Kojève, "Tyranny and Wisdom," in Leo Strauss, *On Tyranny* (Ithaca, N.Y.: Cornell University Press, 1968), 172.

6. Ibid., 156.

7. Ibid., 164. But when Kojève argues that "the duty of the philosopher is to abandon these prejudices as quickly and completely as possible," D&G may part company with him, since prejudices are associated with the plane of immanence on which the philosopher creates concepts.

8. Indeed, according to D&G, figures are common to the sciences—"functives [which characterize the sciences] are not concepts but figures"—and religion, thus making them a specialty of the sage (125).

9. Meier, *The Greek Discovery of Politics,* 117.

10. Ibid., 116.

11. Ibid., 116–17.

12. As Vernant remarks, the "egalitarian order based on the reciprocity of relations" in the polis, and which imposes a common law on all its elements, does not mean that the equilibrium between the powers is static: "it encompassed opposition, it was formed out of conflict. Each force prevailed in turn, seizing power and then falling back, yielding it up in proportion to its earlier advance" (Vernant, *The Origins of Greek Thought,* 123).

13. If with the friend "a vital relationship with the Other" is introduced into thought "that was supposed to have been excluded from pure thought" (4), is the Other, then, not primarily a rival in the struggle in which the friend of wisdom vies with other pretenders?

14. Friedrich Nietzsche, "Homer's Contest," in *On the Genealogy of Morals,* trans. C. Diethe (Cambridge: Cambridge University Press, 2007), 178.

15. Even though D&G allow for the rivalry between equals to turn into enmity, friendship (as the ground for contest) is for them the primary characteristic of Greek citizenship. Yet, it has also been observed that it was the philosophers (Socrates, and especially Aristotle) who opposed *philia* as the "political, noneconomic equalization" of the citizens of the polis to the fierce agonal spirit of all against all that reigned in the polis, which constantly threatened the commonwealth. *Philia* is thus a philosophical desideratum at a time of all-out competition aiming at forming a community to begin with. (See Hannah Arendt, "Socrates," in *The Promise of Politics* [New York: Schocken Books, 2005], 16–17.)

16. See *Philebus* 15a and *Republic* 533d, in Plato, *Collected Dialogues,* 1091 and 765.

17. But this essentially Greek thing that is philosophy also undergoes "evolution or transformations [*mutations*]," and "the list of conceptual personae is never closed" (5). As an aside, let me note that in what Heidegger calls the "new beginning," philosophical thought is supposed to become more Greek than that of the historical Greeks. But to return to *What Is Philosophy?,* the case of Blanchot, who today has taken up again the question of the friend in philosophy and elaborated "on the relationship of friendship with the possibility of thought in the modern world" (219n5), shows that the "new conceptual personae [that he introduces] into the heart of the purest Thought," although "personae [that]

are hardly Greek, arriving from elsewhere as if they had gone through a catastrophe that draws them toward new living relationships raised to the level of a priori characteristics" (4–5), are still, however unheard-of, mutations of the conceptual persona of the friend intrinsic to philosophical thought. Indeed, according to D&G, Blanchot's "friends" represent personae that articulate "a turning away, a certain tiredness, a certain distress between friends that converts friendship itself to thought of the concept as distrust and infinite patience" (5). But, at the same time, in trying to understand the diversity of conceptual personae in philosophy after Greece, one must also be careful, D&G caution, not to reduce them "to the already complex unity of the Greek philosopher" (ibid.).

18. Georg Simmel, "Die Geselligkeit (Beispiel der Reinen oder Formalen Soziologie)," in Georg Simmel, *Gesamtausgabe* (Frankfurt/Main: Suhrkamp, 1999), vol. 16, 103–4.

19. Ibid., p. 106.

20. Ibid., 106–7.

21. Ibid., 110–11.

22. Ibid., 111. For Simmel, parlor games, coquetry, conversation (*Gespräch*), and so forth are aspects of pure sociability whose overall significance he finds realized in such phenomena as the knightly brotherhoods in the German Middle Ages or the court society of the ancien régime.

Chapter 5

1. Friedrich Nietzsche, *The Will to Power,* trans. W. Kaufmann and R. J. Hollingdale (New York: Random House, 1967), 220–21.

2. Raymond Ruyer, *Néo-Finalisme* (Paris: Presses Universitaires de France, 2012), 14.

3. Ibid., 14–15.

4. Immanuel Kant, *Critique of Pure Reason,* 231.

5. Ibid., 232.

6. One is reminded here of Deleuze's reference to cinematographic and philosophical ideas in "What Is the Creative Act?" (Gilles Deleuze, *Two Regimes of Madness: Texts and Interviews 1975–1995,* ed. D. Lapoujade [New York: Semiotexte, 2006], 317–29.)

7. Weil writes: "No Stoic ever contended that all is matter, drawn from matter, or reducible to matter. They teach that nothing exists that does not contain matter, that is, that does not contain both the active and the passive principle. If one is to give such a doctrine a name, it would be more appropriate to use the neologism 'corporalism.'" (Erich Weil, "Le 'matérialisme' des stoïciens," in *Essais et conférences,* vol. 1 [Paris: Vrin, 1991], 110.)

8. Emile Bréhier, "La théorie des incorporels," *Etudes de philosophie antique* (Paris: PUF, 1955), 106.

9. Deleuze and Parnet, *Dialogues II,* 63.

10. Emile Bréhier, *La Théorie des incorporels dans l'ancien stoïcisme* (Paris: Vrin, 1970), 13.

11. Ibid., 12.

12. Deleuze and Parnet, *Dialogues II,* 63. In *What Is Philosophy?* D&G claim that the plane of immanence is "surrounded by illusions," in particular, transcendental illusions, which form "a thick fog around the plane" (49–50). The vapor of the incorporeals, made up by the concepts of philosophy, is one that arises from the plane, whereas the illusions seem to surround it.

13. Deleuze and Parnet, *Dialogues II,* 63–64. It is also in the context of this doctrine that D&G's claim in *What Is Philosophy?* that "the concept is in a state of *survey* [*survol;* overflight, perhaps also in the sense of the cinematographic term "panning," that is, of the rotation of the camera in order to keep a moving object in view] in relation to its components, endlessly traversing them according to an order without distance" (20), needs to be understood.

14. Gilles Deleuze, *Negotiations,* 136. Deleuze adds: "Philosophers introduce new concepts, they explain them, but they don't tell us, not completely anyway, the problems to which those concepts are a response" (ibid.).

15. For an excellent elaboration on the notion of "brain," I refer to Alliez's *The Signature of the World.* The author shows that it is in Alfred North Whitehead's speculative empiricism, that is, in the latter's attempt to understand, in countereffectuation of the Kantian Copernican revolution, the subject on the basis of its objects, that D&G find the notion in question. The brain is another term for a new subject, one that is as physical as its objects, and that in Whitehead's "superior sensualism" constitutes itself ontologically by way of the internal awareness that characterizes all objects and varieties of the universe. "Brain," prior to the "material brain," refers to the "panpsychism" of all things (54–59).

16. With Ilya Progogine and Isabelle Stengers's *Order out of Chaos* in mind, D&G argue in the chapter "Functives and Concepts" that "the pre-Socratics had already grasped the essential point for a determination of science, valid right up to our time, when they made physics a theory of mixtures and their different types" (126–27).

17. Ruyer, *Néo-Finalisme,* 116–17.

18. Ibid., 88.

19. Ibid., 93.

20. Ibid., 126–27.

21. Ibid., 112.

22. Ibid., 120, 132.

23. Ibid., 115, 102.

24. It should also be noted that this stress on "survey" through which a concept folds upon itself, and is, thus, always also a concept of concept, immediately aware of itself in what Alliez has characterized as a "conceptual vitalism," is intimately linked to D&G's rejection of transcendence in all its forms (Alliez, *The Signature of the World,* 84). Indeed, transcendence inhibits from the start all immediate relation to self, all self-experience, if I may call it that, of the concept.

25. Gilles Deleuze and Félix Guattari, *A Thousand Plateaus: Capitalism and Schizophrenia,* trans. B. Massumi (Minneapolis: University of Minnesota Press, 1987), 361.

26. In this context one should also mention D&G's complete horror of "discussion."

27. Deleuze, *Negotiations,* 152.

28. In this context, Deleuze's discussion of communication in "What Is the Creative Act?" is highly illuminating. Indeed in this essay, communication is defined as "the transmission and propagation of information," information, in a nod to Foucault, being determined as "a set of imperatives, slogans, directions—order-words. When you are informed, you are told what you are supposed to believe. In other words, informing means circulating an order-word. Police declarations are appropriately called communiqués. Information is communicated to us, they tell us what we are supposed to be ready to, or have to, or be held to believe." Communication as the transmission of order-words is a characteristic of what Deleuze names, after William Burroughs, "control societies," societies that in the name of universals, I add, no longer have to discipline their citizens, since repression and control are accomplished by way of the information they are fed (Deleuze, "What Is the Creative Act?" 325–26).

29. When Deleuze argues in *Dialogues II* that "what is interesting is the middle [*milieu*]" (39) and that "things do not begin to live except in the middle [*milieu*]" (55), a different use is made of the term. In any case, middle here does not imply "center"; rather, the middle is, as Deleuze suggests, in excess of a center. But does a middle not also presuppose a milieu in the sense of a medium?

30. For this requirement of thought, see François Jullien, *De l'universel, de l'uniforme, du commun et du dialogue entre les cultures* (Paris: Fayard, 2008), 68.

31. "Instituting" renders the French "*instauration,*" which D&G, in an obvious reference to Etienne Souriau's *L'instauration philosophique,* use exclusively when speaking of the plane of immanence. For the difference between the two terms see Leonard Lawlor, "Note on the Relation Between Etienne Souriau's *L'instauration philosophique* and Deleuze and Guattari's *What Is Philosophy?,*" in *Deleuze Studies* 5 (2011): 400–406.

32. Henri Bergson, *An Introduction to Metaphysics,* trans. T. E. Hulme (New York: Macmillan, 1987), 23–24.

33. Ibid., 45, 49–50.

34. Ibid., 51.

35. Ibid., 50.

36. For a fine discussion of intuition in Bergson, see Leonard Lawlor, "Intuition and Duration: An Introduction to Bergson's 'Introduction to Metaphysics,'" in *Phenomenology and Bergsonism,* ed. M. Kelly (London: Palgrave-Macmillan, 2010), 25–41.

37. Bergson, *An Introduction to Metaphysics,* 54, 56.

38. Kathrin Thiele, *The Thought of Becoming: Gilles Deleuze's Poetics of Life* (Berlin: Diaphanes, 2008).

39. Friedrich Nietzsche, "Philosophy During the Tragic Age of the Greeks," in *The Complete Works of Friedrich Nietzsche,* vol. 2 (*Early Greek Philosophy*), trans. M. A. Mügge (New York: Russell and Russell, 1964), 86.

40. Ibid.

41. Ibid.

42. Ibid.

43. Ibid., 86–87.

44. Ibid., 92.

45. Ibid., 86–87.

46. Ibid., 91.

47. Deleuze, too, associates the One-All with Spinoza. See *What Is Philosophy?*, 220n5.

48. In *Negotiations*, Deleuze provides a seemingly different understanding of nonphilosophy when he argues that "concepts involve two other dimensions, percepts and affects" (137), two other dimensions "that amount to philosophy's own nonphilosophical understanding of itself. And philosophy requires nonphilosophical understanding just as much as it requires philosophical understanding" (164; trans. mod.). One is reminded here of Kant's famous statement that "thoughts without content are empty, intuitions without concepts are blind. It is thus just as necessary to make the mind's concepts sensible (i.e., to add an object to them in intuition) as it is to make its intuitions understandable (i.e., to bring them under concepts)" (Kant, *Critique of Pure Reason*, 193–94). In any case, when Deleuze adds in *Negotiations* that one needs not only a philosophical but also a nonphilosophical understanding of concepts and that "philosophy has an essential and positive relation to nonphilosophy" (139–40), he is already gesturing toward the relations of mutual resonance and exchange that take place between the three different forms of thought.

Chapter 6

1. Gilles Deleuze, *Negotiations*, 122.

2. Nietzsche, "Philosophy During the Tragic Age of the Greeks," 90.

3. This pervasive topographical imagery involved in the elementary description of the essence of philosophy is further evidence of the fact that the theme of geophilosophy in *What Is Philosophy?* is not at all a marginal aspect of D&G's philosophy but goes to the very heart of what they understand by philosophy.

4. As we have already seen, European philosophy is geographically diverse.

5. Deleuze and Parnet, *Dialogues II*, 74.

6. Vernant, *The Origins of Greek Thought*, 108.

7. Ibid., 107, 103.

8. Ibid., 107.

9. Friedrich Nietzsche, *Thus Spoke Zarathustra: A Book for Everyone and No One*, trans. R. J. Hollingdale (London: Penguin Books, 2003), 325.

10. See also the wonderful essay by Kathrin Thiele, "'To Believe in This World, As It Is': Immanence and the Quest for Political Activism," in *Deleuze Studies* 4 (2010 supplement): 28–45.

11. Emile Bréhier, "La notion de problème en philosophie," in *Etudes de philosophie antique* (Paris: PUF, 1955).

12. Simmel, "Die Geselligkeit," 115–16.

13. Martin Heidegger, *Basic Concepts of Aristotelian Philosophy*, trans. R. D. Metcalf and M. B. Tanzer (Bloomington: Indiana University Press, 2009), 74–75.

14. Marcel Detienne, *The Masters of Truth in Archaic Greece,* 109.

15. Ibid., 111.

16. Ibid.

17. Ibid., 114.

18. Ibid., 116.

19. Ibid., 115.

20. Ibid.

21. Ibid.

22. Gottfried Wilhelm Friedrich Hegel, "Who Thinks Abstractly?," in *Hegel: Texts and Commentaries,* ed. and trans. W. Kaufmann (Garden City, N.Y.: Doubleday, 1965), 113–18.

23. About recognition, D&G state that, of all the finite movements of thought, it "is certainly the one that goes the least far and is the most impoverished and puerile" (139).

24. Nietzsche writes that "through thus selecting and precipitating the unusual, astounding, difficult, and divine, Philosophy marks the boundary-lines dividing her from Science in the same way as she does it from Prudence by emphasizing the useless" (Nietzsche, "Philosophy During the Tragic Age of the Greeks," 90). It also needs to be pointed out that these categories of the Interesting, Remarkable, and Important are essentially Early Romantic conceptions.

Chapter 7

1. Sissa and Detienne, *The Daily Life of the Greek Gods,* 141.

2. Ibid., 142.

3. Ibid., 221.

4. Burkert, *Homo Necans,* 148, 157. A couple of sentences later, he writes: "At the city's highest point, atop the Acropolis, there is also that bit of sea that surfaces in the sanctuary" (157).

5. Sissa and Detienne, *The Daily Life of the Greek Gods,* 220–21.

6. Ibid., 221.

7. Burkert, *Homo Necans,* 149.

8. Indeed, the sentence is also somewhat ambiguous in the original, since the lack of a conjunction, "and," makes one read it as if the maritime component went under the sea, which makes little sense. For the importance that Deleuze attributes to the conjunction "and" as opposed to the verb "is," see Deleuze and Parnet, *Dialogues II,* 9–10, 58–59.

9. James Gleick, *Chaos: Making a New Science* (New York: Penguin Books, 2008), 96–100.

10. François Lefèvre, *Histoire du monde grecque* (Paris: Librairie Générale Française, 2007), 39.

11. This fractal nature and its exposure in all places to the sea distinguish Greece fundamentally from China, for example. In Greece the other is virtually present in all its locations. After elaborating on the image of water in Chinese thought, François Jullien, who certainly cannot be accused of any partiality with respect to the West, writes: "In China, there really was no elsewhere to which to

sail. In Greece, in contrast, the sea is everywhere, infiltrating the land on every side and breaking into it; its ever heaving 'back' is a place where adventures are always possible not only for a sailor but likewise for a military strategist or a philosopher. Odysseus, seeking Return, yet drifting toward the unknown, was already, if not the first philosopher, then the father of philosophy.

"In China, the sea borders the earth at the lowest point of a downward slope. It does not encourage one to set out across it; it is neither threatening, nor does it lure one on to confront its dangers. It does not encourage thought to become *deterritorialized.* Immanence is not presented by it as a 'level,' with the sea 'cutting through chaos' (Deleuze). Rather, it appears as a great fund (of the processivity of Things). So there is no reason for the general to risk setting out to cross it. Nor is the sage in any doubt on that score." (François Jullien, *A Treatise on Efficacy: Between Western and Chinese Thinking,* trans. J. Lloyd [Honolulu: University of Hawai'i Press, 2004], 183.)

12. Jean-François Mattéi, *Le Procès de l'Europe: Grandeur et misère de la culture européenne* (Paris: Presses Universitaires de France, 2011), 96.

13. D&G cite Jean-Pierre Faye but should have cited the latter's sources: primarily Heidegger and Beaufret.

14. Jean-François Mattéi, *L'Etranger et le simulacre: Essai sur la fondation de l'ontologie platonicienne* (Paris: Presses Universitaires de France, 1983). See also Mattéi, *Le Procès de l'Europe,* 87–88.

15. Henri Joly, *Etudes platoniciennes: La question des étrangers* (Paris: Vrin, 1992), 95, 13.

16. Herodotus, *The Histories,* trans. A. de Selincourt (Harmondsworth, U.K.: Penguin Classics, 1972), 489. Herodotus speaks in Book IV, 46, of *aporois prosmisgein,* "impossible to come to close quarters with," and in Book IX, 49, of *prospheresthai aporoi,* impossible to surround, or "not easy to come to grips with" as A. de Selincourt translates (597).

Chapter 8

1. Vernant, *The Origins of Greek Thought,* 107.

2. Ibid., 126 (emphasis in the original).

3. This is again a distinction that is largely indebted to Nietzsche's "Philosophy During the Tragic Age of the Greeks." Indeed, Nietzsche contends that Heraclitus's conception of the cosmic war of opposites is "drawn from the purest source of Hellenism, which considers the struggle as the continual sway of a homogeneous, severe justice bound by eternal laws. Only a Greek was able to consider this conception as the fundament of a *Cosmodicy;* it is Hesiod's good Eris transfigured into the cosmic principle, it is the idea of a contest, an idea held by individual Greeks and by their State, and translated out of the gymnasia and palaestra, out of the artistic agonistic, out of the struggle of the political parties and out of the towns into the most general principle, so that the machinery of the universe is regulated by it" (Nietzsche, "Philosophy During the Tragic Age of the Greeks," 101–2).

4. Carl Schmitt, *Der Nomos der Erde im Völkerrecht des Jus Publicum Europaeum* (Berlin: Duncker and Humblot, 1988), 36–51.

5. Something similar is the case when "the pre-Socratics treat physical elements like concepts: they take them for themselves, independently of any reference" (90–91).

6. For Heidegger, too, the claim that philosophy is Greek means that it is atheist. To speak of Christian philosophy, for example, is for him a contradiction in terms.

7. In the original, "Earth" is capitalized.

8. Nietzsche, "Philosophy During the Tragic Age of the Greeks," 81, 76; the reference to the ambiance, or atmosphere, that Greece provided for philosophy is from Friedrich Nietzsche, "On the Uses and Disadvantages of History for Life," in *Untimely Meditations,* trans. R. J. Hollingdale (Cambridge: Cambridge University Press, 1983), 63–64.

9. Nietzsche, "Philosophy During the Tragic Age of the Greeks," 112.

10. Deleuze and Parnet, *Dialogues II,* 49.

11. Nietzsche, *The Will to Power,* 377.

12. In the original, "Earth" is capitalized.

13. Gilles Deleuze, *Difference and Repetition,* trans. P. Patton (New York: Columbia University Press, 1994), 29.

14. "Libres propos de Jean Beaufret," 92–93. The reference to "the few other great beginnings" is to Martin Heidegger, "Hölderlin's Earth and Heaven," in *Elucidations of Hölderlin's Poetry,* trans. K. Hoeller (Amherst, N.Y.: Prometheus Books, 2000), 201.

15. "Libres propos de Jean Beaufret," 92–93.

Chapter 9

1. Gilles Deleuze, *Essays Critical and Clinical,* trans. D. W. Smith and M. A. Greco (Minneapolis: University of Minnesota Press, 1997), 137.

2. In *Negotiations* Spinoza is described as "the absolute philosopher," and "the most philosophical of philosophers, the purest in some sense" (Deleuze, *Negotiations,* 140, 165).

3. François Jullien, *De l'Universel, de l'uniforme, du commun et du dialogue entre les cultures* (Paris: Fayard, 2008), 252.

4. Gilles Deleuze, *Proust and Signs,* trans. R. Howard (London: Athlone Press, 2000), 163.

5. It is, of course, the case that D&G refer to religion, history, and especially to logic. All three are in different ways functions of opinion. In the latter case, it is clear from the beginning of chapter 6 that the task of logic consists precisely in undermining the constitutive differences between the tasks of philosophy and the sciences and that its ultimate aim is to supplant philosophy.

Bibliography

Alliez, Eric. *The Signature of the World, or What Is Deleuze and Guattari's Philosophy?* Trans. E. R. Albert and A. Toscano. New York: Continuum, 2004.

Arendt, Hannah. "Socrates." In *The Promise of Politics,* 5–39. New York: Schocken Books, 2005.

Aristotle. *Complete Works.* Edited by J. Barnes. Princeton: Princeton University Press, 1985.

Beaufret, Jean. "La naissance de la philosophie." In *Dialogue avec Heidegger: Philosophie grecque,* 19–37. Paris: Minuit, 1973.

Bergson, Henri. *An Introduction to Metaphysics.* Trans. T. E. Hulme. New York: Macmillan, 1987.

Blanchot, Maurice. *The Space of Literature.* Trans. A. Smock. Lincoln: University of Nebraska Press, 1982.

Bonta, Mark, and John Protevi. *Deleuze and Geophilosophy: A Guide and a Glossary.* Edinburgh: Edinburgh University Press, 2006.

Braudel, Fernand. *La Méditerranée et le monde méditerranéen à l'époque de Philippe II,* 2nd edition. Paris: Colin, 1960.

Bréhier, Emile. "La notion de problème en philosophie." In *Etudes de philosophie antique,* 10–16. Paris: Presses Universitaires de France, 1955.

———. "La théorie des incorporels." In *Etudes de philosophie antique,* 105–16. Paris: Presses Universitaires de France, 1955.

———. *La théorie des incorporels dans l'ancien stoïcisme.* Paris: Vrin, 1970.

Burkert, Walter. *Homo Necans: The Anthropology of Ancient Greek Sacrificial Ritual and Myth.* Trans. P. Bing. Berkeley: University of California Press, 1983.

Cohen, Jack, and Ian Stewart. *The Collapse of Chaos: Discovering Simplicity in a Complex World.* New York: Viking, 1994.

Cross, Donald. "What Is Nonstyle in *What Is Philosophy?*" In *Deleuze and the Schizoanalysis of Literature,* eds. I. Buchanan, A. Tynan, and T. Matts. New York: Bloomsbury Academic (forthcoming 2014).

Deleuze, Gilles. *Difference and Repetition.* Trans. P. Patton. New York: Columbia University Press, 1994.

———. *Essays Critical and Clinical.* Trans. D. W. Smith and M. A. Greco. Minneapolis: University of Minnesota Press, 1997.

———. *Negotiations 1972–1990.* Trans. M. Joughin. New York: Columbia University Press, 1995.

———. *Proust and Signs.* Trans. R. Howard. London: Athlone Press, 2000.

———. "Remarques." In *Nos Grecs et leurs modernes,* 249–50. Ed. B. Cassin, Paris: Seuil, 1992.

———. "Théorie des multiplicités chez Bergson." http://www.le-terrier.net/deleuze/20bergson.htm.

———. "What Is the Creative Act?" In *Two Regimes of Madness: Texts and Interviews 1975–1995,* trans. A. Hodge and M. Taormina, 317–29. New York: Semiotexte, 2006.

Deleuze, Gilles, and Félix Guattari. *Anti-Oedipus: Capitalism and Schizophrenia.* Trans. R. Hurley, M. Seem, and H. R. Lane. New York: Viking Press, 1977.

———. *Kafka: Toward a Minor Literature.* Trans. D. Polan. Minneapolis: University of Minnesota Press, 1986.

———. *Qu'est-ce que la philosophie?* Paris: Minuit, 1991.

———. *A Thousand Plateaus: Capitalism and Schizophrenia.* Trans. B. Massumi. Minneapolis: University of Minnesota Press, 1987.

———. *What Is Philosophy?* Trans. H. Tomlinson and G. Burchell. New York: Columbia University Press, 1994.

Deleuze, Gilles, and Claire Parnet. *Dialogues II.* Trans. H. Tomlinson and B. Habberjam. New York: Columbia University Press, 2002.

Detienne, Marcel. "Apollon Archégète: Un modèle politique de la territorialisation." In *Tracés de fondation,* ed. M. Detienne, 301–11. Louvain-Paris: Peeters, 1990.

———. *The Masters of Truth in Archaic Greece.* Trans. J. Lloyd. New York: Zone Books, 1996.

———. "Qu'est-ce qu'un site?" In *Tracés de fondation,* ed. M. Detienne, 1–16. Louvain-Paris: Peeters, 1990.

Detienne, Marcel, and Giulia Sissa. *The Daily Life of the Greek Gods.* Trans. J. Lloyd. Stanford, Calif.: Stanford University Press, 2000.

Dosse, François. *Gilles Deleuze and Félix Guattari: Intersecting Lives.* Trans. D. Glassman. New York: Columbia University Press, 2010.

Gleick, James. *Chaos: Making a New Science.* New York: Penguin Books, 2008.

Grimal, Pierre. *The Dictionary of Classical Mythology.* Trans. A. R. Maxwell-Hyslop. Oxford: Basil Blackwell, 1986.

Günzel, Stephan. "'Geschichtlicher Boden': Nachphänomenologische Geophilosophie bei Heidegger und Deleuze." In *Phänomenologische Forschungen,* eds. E. W. Orth and K.-H. Lembeck, 51–85. Hamburg: Felix Meiner Verlag 2002.

———. "Nietzsches Geophilosophie und die 'gemässigte Klimazone' im Denken des Abendlandes." *Dialektik,* no.1 (2000): 17–34.

Hegel, Gottfried Wilhelm Friedrich. *Philosophy of Right.* Trans. T. M. Knox. Oxford: Oxford University Press, 1952.

———. "Who Thinks Abstractly?" In *Hegel: Texts and Commentaries,* trans. W. Kaufmann, 113–18. Garden City, N.Y.: Doubleday, 1965.

Heidegger, Martin. *Basic Concepts of Aristotelian Philosophy.* Trans. R. D. Metcalf and M. B. Tanzer. Bloomington: Indiana University Press, 2009.

———. *Elucidations of Hölderlin's Poetry.* Trans. K. Hoeller. Amherst, N.Y.: Prometheus Books, 2000.

———. *Introduction to Metaphysics.* Trans. G. Fried and R. Polt. New Haven, Conn.: Yale University Press, 2000.

Herodotus. *The Histories.* Trans. A. de Sélincourt. Harmondsworth, U.K.: Penguin Classics, 1972.

Hesiod. *The Homeric Hymns and Homerica.* Trans. H. G. Evelyn-White. Cambridge, Mass.: Harvard University Press, 1959.

Jullien, François. *De l'universel, de l'uniforme, du commun et du dialogue entre les cultures.* Paris: Fayard, 2008.

———. *A Treatise on Efficacy: Between Western and Chinese Thinking.* Trans. J. Lloyd. Honolulu: University of Hawai'i Press, 2004.

Joly, Henri. *Etudes platoniciennes: La question des étrangers.* Paris: Vrin, 1992.

Kant, Immanuel. *Critique of Pure Reason.* Trans. P. Guyer and A. W. Wood. Cambridge: Cambridge University Press, 1998.

Kojève, Alexandre. "Tyranny and Wisdom." In Leo Strauss, *On Tyranny,* 143–88. Ithaca, N.Y.: Cornell University Press, 1968.

Lawlor, Leonard. "Intuition and Duration: An Introduction to Bergson's 'Introduction to Metaphysics.'" In *Phenomenology and Bergsonism,* ed. M. Kelly, 25–41. London: Palgrave-Macmillan, 2010.

———. "A Note on the Relation Between Etienne Souriau's *L'instauration philosophique* and Deleuze and Guattari's *What Is Philosophy?*" *Deleuze Studies* 5 (2011): 400–406.

Lefèvre, François. *Histoire du monde grec antique.* Paris: Librairie Général Française, 2007.

Liddell, Henry George, and Robert Scott. *A Greek-English Lexicon.* Oxford: Oxford University Press, 1968.

Loraux, Nicole. *Born of the Earth: Myth and Politics in Athens.* Trans. S. Stewart. Ithaca, N.Y.: Cornell University Press, 2000.

———. *The Children of Athena: Athenian Ideas About Citizenship and the Division Between the Sexes.* Trans. C. Levine. Princeton, N.J.: Princeton University Press, 1993.

———. "Clisthène, diviseur-lieur d'Athènes." In *L'inactuel: Psychanalyse & Culture* 8 (special issue on "Territoires, frontières, passages"), 5–27. Paris: Calmann-Levy, 1997.

———. *The Invention of Athens: The Funeral Oration in the Classical City.* Trans. A. Sheridan. Cambridge, Mass.: Harvard University Press, 1986.

Mattéi, Jean-François. *L'Etranger et le simulacre: Essai sur la fondation de l'ontologie platonicienne.* Paris: Presses Universitaires de France, 1983.

———. *Le Procès de l'Europe: Grandeur et misère de la culture européenne.* Paris: Presses Universitaires de France, 2011.

Meier, Christian. *The Greek Discovery of Politics.* Trans. D. McLintock. Cambridge, Mass.: Harvard University Press, 1990.

Nietzsche, Friedrich. *Beyond Good and Evil: Prelude to a Philosophy of the Future.* Trans. W. Kaufmann. New York: Vintage Books, 1989.

———. "Homer's Contest." In *The Complete Works of Friedrich Nietzsche,* vol. 2 (*Early Greek Philosophy*), trans. M. A. Mügge, 49–62. New York: Russell and Russell, 1964.

———. "On the Uses and Disadvantages of History for Life." In *Untimely Meditations,* trans. R. J. Hollingdale, 57–123. Cambridge, Mass.: Cambridge University Press.

———. "Philosophy During the Tragic Age of the Greeks." In *The Complete Works of Friedrich Nietzsche,* Vol. 2 (*Early Greek Philosophy*), trans. M. A. Mügge, 71–170. New York: Russell and Russell, 1964.

———. *Thus Spoke Zarathustra: A Book for Everyone and No One.* Trans. R. J. Hollingdale. London: Penguin Books, 2003.

———. *The Will to Power.* Trans. W. Kaufmann and R. J. Hollingdale. New York: Random House, 1967.

Patton, Paul. *Deleuzian Concepts: Philosophy, Colonization, Politics.* Stanford, Calif.: Stanford University Press, 2010.

Plato. *Collected Dialogues.* Trans. E. Hamilton and H. Cairns. Princeton, N.J.: Princeton University Press, 1980.

Renan, Ernest. *Souvenirs d'enfance et de jeunesse.* Paris: Calmann Lévy, 1893.

Ruyer, Raymond. *Néo-Finalisme.* Paris: Presses Universitaires de France, 2012.

Schmitt, Carl. *Der Nomos der Erde im Völkerrecht des Jus Publicum Europaeum.* Berlin: Duncker and Humblot, 1988.

Shapiro, Gary. "Beyond Peoples and Fatherlands: Nietzsche's Geophilosophy and the Direction of the Earth." *Journal of Nietzsche Studies,* nos. 35–36 (2008): 9–27.

Simmel, Georg. "Die Geselligkeit (Beispiel der Reinen oder Formalen Soziologie)." In Georg Simmel, *Gesamtausgabe,* vol. 16, 103–21. Frankfurt/Main: Suhrkamp, 1999.

Somers-Hall, Henry. *Hegel, Deleuze, and the Critique of Representation: Dialectics of Negation and Difference.* Albany: State University of New York Press, 2012.

Thiele, Kathrin. "'To Believe in This World, As It Is': Immanence and the Quest for Political Activism." *Deleuze Studies* 4, supplement (2010): 28–45.

———. *The Thought of Becoming: Gilles Deleuze's Poetics of Life.* Berlin: Diaphanes, 2008.

Towarnicki, Frédéric de. "Libres propos de Jean Beaufret." *Ethernité* 1, no. 1, 91–97. Paris: Editions de la Différence, 1985.

Vernant, Jean-Pierre. *The Origins of Greek Thought.* Ithaca, N.Y.: Cornell University Press, 1982.

Weil, Erich. "Le 'matérialisme' des stoïciens." In *Essais et conférences,* vol. 1, 106–23. Paris: Vrin, 1991.

Index